SERIES EDITOR: LEE JOHI

**OSPREY MILITARY WARRIOR**

# BRITISH REDCOAT
## 1740-1793

TEXT BY
## STUART REID

COLOUR BY
## RICHARD HOOK

First published in Great Britain in 1996 by Osprey Publishing, Elms Court, Chapel Way, Botley, Oxford OX2 9LP, United Kingdom.

ISBN 1 85532 554 3

Military Editor: Iain MacGregor
Designed by TT Designs

Filmset in Great Britain
Printed through World Print Ltd., Hong Kong

FOR A CATALOGUE OF ALL BOOKS PUBLISHED BY OSPREY MILITARY, AUTOMOTIVE AND AVIATION PLEASE WRITE TO:

**The Marketing Manager, Osprey Publishing, PO Box 140, Wellingborough, Northants, NN8 4ZA, United Kingdom**

VISIT OSPREY'S WEBSITE AT:

http://www.osprey-publishing.co.uk

# Dedication and thanks

To Susan for taking the photographs.

# Editor's note

Readers may notice the inclusion within the plates, and accompanying text, of material relating to David Morier's paintings of British Grenadiers stationed at Roermond, commonly dated at 1751. The author has previously covered this topic in the first volume of the Men-at-Arms title *King George's Army 1740-93*, explaining the significance of some of the paintings being completed in 1748, and not 1751 as originally thought.

# Publishers' note

Readers may wish to study this title in conjunction with the following Osprey publications:

MAA  39 *British Army in North America 1775-1801*
MAA  48 *Wolfe's Army*
MAA 118 *The Jacobite Rebellions 1689-1745*
MAA 224 *French Army in the American War of Independence*
MAA 273 *General Washington's Army 1775-1778: 1*
MAA 285 *King George's Army 1740-93: 1*
MAA 289 *King George's Army 1740-93: 2*
MAA 290 *General Washington's Army 1775-1778: 2*
MAA 292 *King George's Army 1740-93: 3*
MAA 296 *Louis XV's Army (1) Cavalry*
CAM 12 *Culloden 1746*
CAM 37 *Boston 1775*

# BRITISH REDCOAT
# 1740-1793

## INTRODUCTION

During the 50-year period covered by this study, the British army earned itself a formidable reputation as a fighting force and laid the foundations of one of the greatest empires in history. It was however a profoundly unpopular institution at the time, and formed from a far lower proportion of the population than almost any other army in Europe. A combination of popular distrust of an organisation chiefly employed at home as a police force and its demonisation in American mythology has created a popular image of the army as being little removed from a penal institution – a walking concentration camp run by aristocratic dilettantes.

The reality was very different, and the purpose of this study is to portray the ordinary British infantry soldier as he really was, rather than the grotesque caricature created largely by American propaganda.

First it may be helpful to outline the nature of the organisation in which the Redcoat served.

That organisation varied throughout the period according to short-term Treasury policy and whether a regiment was carried on the British or Irish Establishment. Prior to 1770, regiments stationed in Ireland were normally maintained only at cadre strength, but after that date the two Establishments were harmonised. Infantry regiments normally comprised only a single battalion of nine or ten companies. Each company was run by three commissioned officers – a captain, a lieutenant and an ensign, who form no part of this study, and three sergeants, three corporals, two drummers and, depending upon circumstances, anything between 30 and 70 – or occasionally 100 – private sentinels.

## RECRUITMENT

Most recruits were young men, frequently teenagers and almost invariably unmarried at the time of enlistment. Few of those who joined the army in the 18th century recorded their reasons for doing so, but the most basic motivation was probably economic: whatever its disadvantages, the army would at least promise a relatively secure source of food, shelter and clothing. Recruiters would certainly take advantage of periodic economic recessions that afflicted the clothing industry to sign on out-of-work weavers or other cloth workers. However, for the most part, recruits seem to have been youths picked up at country fairs or after the harvest.

ABOVE **Highland soldier as depicted for Major George Grant's** *Highland Military Discipline.* **[Author]**

ABOVE LEFT **Reconstruction, 13th Foot c.1745, which successfully captures the rather scruffy appearance of soldiers on service. The large quantity of facial hair may appear surprising, but one of Barrell's grenadiers, as depicted by David Morier, has an equally heavy beard. [Author's collection]**

ABOVE RIGHT **Rear view of the same soldier, providing a good view of the hairy duffle-bag style knapsack. One of Morier's Culloden paintings depicts the officers and men of the 13th wearing black gaiters rather than the white ones shown here. [Author's collection]**

Although older, married agricultural workers could normally hope for at least a certain degree of stability in their working lives, it was a very different story for the young and unskilled casual labourer. The best he could expect was to be taken on by a farmer for six months or perhaps a year at a time. If master and man agreed well enough, the engagement might continue, ultimately allowing him to marry and settle down. Otherwise it was customary to seek fresh employment at one of the traditional hiring fairs, and no fair was complete without at least one, and usually two or three, predatory army recruiting parties ready to snap up men who were unable to find a new master or those who were simply bored and fed up with the unceasing grind of farm work.

One of the verses in an old recruiting song for the 42nd Highlanders is quite explicit about this particular motive:

*It's in by the barn and it's out by the byre,*
*This auld farmer thinks you'll never tire,*
*It's a slavery job, o' low degree,*
*So 'list my bonnie laddie and come alang wi' me.*

Another often quite important factor, still encountered today, was peer pressure. On 22 December 1751 Captain Archibald Grant wrote from Leeds: 'Last Tuesday being Mercat day I inlisted four very good Recruits, in my opinion all Shoemakers in this Town, they came together in a body and told me that if I would take them all they would Enlist but they were determined not to separate.'

There were, of course, others who had more pressing reasons, both legal and domestic, for enlisting – pregnant girlfriends being a timeless classic.

While it is quite easy to be cynical about the motives impelling recruits, there is no real reason to doubt that at the end of the day the great majority of volunteers for the British army in the 18th century were drawn by the promise of an easy life and military glory. This is not to say that they were all naive enough to be taken in by false, or at best exaggerated, promises, but rather that they were attracted by a vision of something more exciting than labouring from dawn to dusk for the rest of their lives in the parish where they had been born.

Certain categories of men could not, in theory at least, be enlisted into his majesty's service. Apart from the obviously ruptured and lame, these included Roman Catholics, indentured servants and apprentices, and members of the militia. Others, depending upon how choosy the recruiters could afford to be, might include sailors and colliers – both notoriously prone to bronchial and tubercular diseases – and the usual crowd of petty criminals and vagabonds whom the local authorities were usually keen to wish upon the army. At the end of the day, though, the only real qualifications for a soldier were that he should be at least 5ft 6in tall (or thought likely to grow to it), sound in mind and limb, and prepared to swear before a magistrate that he was indeed a Protestant and not afflicted by anything else which might debar him from serving.

There were also a fair number of men who found themselves in the army through no choice of their own. General conscription did not exist as such, but in times of crisis Parliament was prone to passing temporary Acts allowing local authorities to impress an alarmingly broad range of men. Generally known as 'vestry men', they could include every petty criminal for miles around. Such involuntary recruits were very much a mixed blessing and hardly served to raise the status of soldiers. After the battle of Culloden, in 1746, the vestry men rounded up for that particular emergency were either employed in prisoner handling or else discharged with almost indecent haste.

ABOVE **Reconstruction: Corporal, 13th Foot c.1748. Note the much trimmer appearance with the coat-skirts turned back and the waistbelt worn under the coat. The dirty smudge on the right knee shows that he has been kneeling to fire in the front rank. [Author's collection]**

## 'Taking the shilling'

Ordinarily, the process of becoming a soldier could be quite a lengthy one. The first point of contact was obviously with a member of a recruiting party. Generally this was the sergeant in charge, since the officer's job was basically to keep an eye on the money and to smooth matters with the local magistrates. A bounty of several pounds was offered to all recruits, but the amount actually paid was a matter for negotiation. Just as a man would haggle with a farmer over his 'fee', he would expect to negotiate with the recruiting sergeant. If less than the authorised sum was eventually agreed, the sergeant and his officer would expect to split the difference. However, if recruits were difficult to come by, it might be necessary to pay over the odds, which bit into their anticipated profit.

Once the bargain was struck, the recruit traditionally received a shilling. Equally traditionally, this was turned into ale at the earliest opportunity. Then he was given a fairly basic medical examination and taken before a magistrate or justice of the peace, who attested him – that is, administered the oath, after which he was considered to be subject to military law as defined by the annual Mutiny Act.

The next step was to march the would-be hero either up to regimental headquarters, where he would be approved or rejected by the commanding officer. If the regiment was serving overseas, he would be taken to its rendezvous. In wartime, this was normally an 'additional company' staffed by officers drawn from the half-pay list. If the officer in charge of the company considered the recruit suitable, he would be taken from there and passed on to one of the depots or stations established for training and exercising of recruits prior to their being shipped overseas. There they would be signed as 'Recruits passed by Field Officers,

BELOW **Pikeman demonstrating 'Charge your pike' in De Geyhn's 1607 *Exercise of Arms*. Note the very close resemblance between this posture and Bland's 'Charge your bayonets'.** [Author's collection]

who will have instructions to inspect them, will be deemed as approved by the Regiment'.

Although there were often complaints about the quality of men recruited for the army in the 18th century, there were in fact some quite daunting financial penalties which normally served to filter out the more unsuitable candidates. However, in wartime these were often disregarded in the desperate scramble to find enough men.

If a man turned out the morning after 'taking the shilling' to be physically unsound or otherwise unsuitable to serve his king, the recruiting sergeant lost the money which had been expended in persuading him to enlist. Similarly, if a man was rejected when he reached the regiment, the officer in charge of the recruiting party lost all the money spent on him up until that point. If he was accepted by the regiment but then rejected by an inspecting general, it was the regiment which suffered. Since by that time he would have been paid or at least credited with his bounty and issued with some of his clothing and equipment, the loss was relatively large.

In theory, a soldier could demand his bounty as a lump sum in cash, and it was quite common for Highland recruits, in particular, to remit the bounty home to their parents. Normally, however, it took the form of a paper transaction and was credited to the soldier's individual account from which deductions were in due course made for his 'necessaries'. Normally these included his knapsack, various extra items of clothing such as shirts and stockings, and more mundane items such as clothes brushes and the blackballs needed for cleaning his boots.

James Aytoun, who enlisted in the 58th Foot at Edinburgh in January 1786, considered himself quite fortunate in this regard: 'I received £1 11s 6d bounty and as I had plenty of shirts, Quartermaster Sergeant Elliott only bought for me out of my bounty two pairs of good shoes at five shillings a pair and two pairs of good, white stockings at two shillings per pair.'

## PAY AND SUBSISTENCE

For most of the period pay was a princely eightpence per day, of which sixpence was accounted subsistence and the remaining tuppence the 'off reckonings' which – less certain administrative deductions – were made over directly to the colonel of the regiment and used by him to pay for most of the soldier's clothing. Any surplus left over was the colonel's perquisite.

Clothing is discussed more fully in *MAA 289: King George's Army (2)*, but essentially a soldier was entitled to a complete suit of clothing annually. It comprised a coat, waistcoat or waistcoat front, breeches, hat, stockings, shoes and a couple of shirts – paid for out of his 'off reckonings'. Any additional items of clothing, which could range from fatigue jackets to additional shirts, gaiters, stockings and shoes, were then paid for through stoppages from his subsistence.

The only time a soldier might actually hope to finger any of the 'off reckonings' was when the clothing to which he was entitled was not delivered for any reason, or was of a lower standard than usual. An example of this was when the short jackets were substituted for the usual heavy regimental coat for service in the West Indies. In this instance, the soldier was entitled to have a 'refund' of 1s 9d.

## Daily Rates of Pay and Subsistence, 1740

| | British Establishment | | Irish Establishment | |
|---|---|---|---|---|
| | *Pay* | *Subs* | *Pay* | *Subs* |
| Sergeant | 1s 6d | 1s 0d | 1s 6d | 1s 0d |
| Corporal | 1s 0d | 8d | 1s 0d | 9d |
| Drummer | 1s 0d | 8d | 1s 0d | 8d |
| Private | 8d | 6d | 7d | 5d |

The subsistence portion of the soldier's pay was, in theory, issued every two months to the regiment. In practice it would then be passed on to the soldier weekly or at shorter or longer intervals if the circumstances demanded it. Out of the 3s 6d subsistence due a soldier each week, his captain was normally authorised to deduct sixpence 'for shoes, stockings, gayters, medicines, shaving, mending of arms, loss by exchange of remittance of their pay but nothing else except such things as may be lost or spoiled by the soldier's negligence and the captain is to accompt with them for the residue every two months'.

Whether any 'residue' from these stoppages actually became available was, of course, a different matter entirely, as James Aytoun, who had the misfortune to be drafted into the badly run 30th Foot, recalled: 'I have to observe that no man, or at least very few that died in Dominique, was out of debt in the company's books. The men's account was never settled nor arrears paid off more than once in six months and frequently on a longer period. It was always observed that a careful soldier was severely watched by the adjutant and pay sergeants, more so than a prodigal, because the prodigal took from the pay sergeant shirts, shoes etc. at an extravagant price and sold the same for less than half their value. In doing so they were rarely out of debt to the pay sergeant. Officers of company seldom gave themselves any concern about their company's accounts. The pay sergeants were heirs at law and, as already observed, most men when dead were in debt in the company's book. It was very easy making a dead man "debtor to

TOP 'Charge your bayonet breast high' – the 2nd Motion.
ABOVE 'Push your bayonet'.

balance"... Adjutant Russell was a mean tyrant. He fixed malignant eye on the best men in the regiment. On one occasion, when told by Sergeant Thomson that one man in the company always received the arrears in full and supplied himself with shirts etc, said our redoubtable adjutant, "Why do you not get him flogged?"'

It is hard to say how typical Aytoun's experience was. It is equally clear that in the better-run units it was quite common to allow the men to purchase their necessaries for themselves instead of stopping the cost out of their subsistence. Nevertheless this was regarded as a privilege rather than a right. On 20 April 1761, for example, the commanding officer of the 42nd Highlanders directed that certain items, including black ribbons for new cockades, needed to be procured. Normally they would have been paid for out of the weekly stoppages, but: 'It is however left to the Commanding Officer of Companys to allow such men as they can depend upon to provide these articles for themselves.'

The remaining three shillings of the soldier's basic pay – plus any additional money which he might earn when off duty, or engaged in roadwork or other exceptional fatigues – had to cover the cost of all his food and drink.

If it was practicable to do so – for example, when a regiment was marching from one quarter to another within the British Isles – he would be given his daily subsistence in hard cash and allowed to purchase whatever he required either from civilian markets or from the sutlers who usually accompanied an army. This was not always possible on active service, of course, or on board a

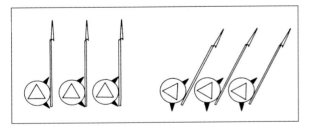

ABOVE **Bayonet drill – 'Culloden variant':** The three soldiers on the left are charging their bayonets in the normal way, standing at a right angle to the enemy, with feet set squarely apart. The three soldiers on the right are thrusting to their right instead of straight ahead. The left foot has not moved and the change in direction is accomplished simply by moving the right foot half a pace backwards.

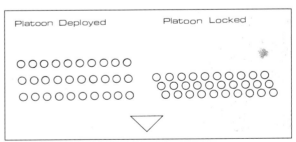

ABOVE **Locking:** The platoon on the left is deployed in the usual order – according to the 1728 regulations half a pace distance between files and two paces between ranks. The platoon on the right has locked up in order to fire a volley. As soon as it has been delivered, the men will step back to leave a two-pace interval between ranks before reloading.

transport. In the latter case the soldier was provided with rations and the cost of them was deducted as a further stoppage.

Normally he was then entitled to receive one pound of bread and either one pound of beef or nine ounces of pork each day, together with lesser quantities of 'small rations' – usually oatmeal, butter or cheese, pease and occasionally rice.

Like most soldiers, James Aytoun was actually much less concerned with strong drink than with food, and his memoirs cover the subject in some detail. In 1786, while still a recruit with the 58th Foot, he describes how, while quartered in Ireland, a butcher in his mess and some other men would periodically buy a sheep which 'when killed and all counted, cost us about 1d per lb'. Others would sometimes visit Downpatrick market to purchase oatmeal for the breakfast porridge. On the other hand, on Dominica, where he served with the 30th Foot, rations were issued, but were rarely consumed by the soldiers themselves: 'We sold all our butter, rice, pease and beef and part of our pork and bought green plantains, vegetables and roast coffee and treacle and made a shift to have a jug of coffee and a piece of bread for breakfast and an ounce or two of pork for dinner with a plate of tolerable good broth made from the salt pork. . . Any supper or third meal we had was a little pork brine, Cayenne pepper and the remainder of our bread.'

How much was actually stopped from the soldier's subsistence in order to pay for these rations varied according to circumstances, but an effort was always made to ensure that at least some hard cash was delivered over to him. Normally this would be paid in local currency; in July 1759, troops in the camp at Lake George in Upper New York were informed: 'The commanding officers of Regiments having been assembled to take into consideration the most convenient method of paying the troops as also weekly stoppages to be made to enable the Captains to provide a necessary supply of shirts shoes & etc. for their Compy. The Genl. directs the payment to be made in the following manner – a Sergt. six shillings, a Corpl. four shillings, Drummer four

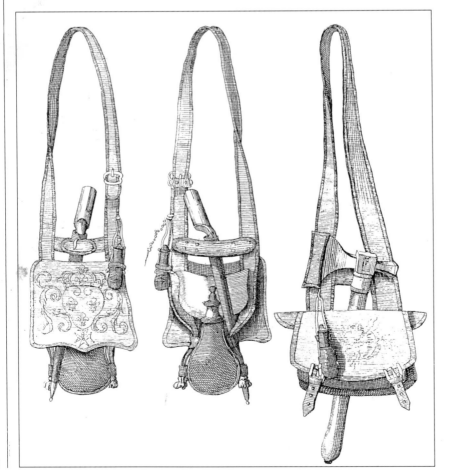

BELOW **French infantry equipment of the early 18th century. Note the small priming flask. Use of such flasks was included in Bland's drill, but in practice probably abandoned by the 1740s. [Author's collection]**

10

shillings, Private Soldiers three shillings per week New York Currency. Eight shillings that currancy being equal to a dollar at 4s & 8d sterling.'

Having arranged for the soldier to receive at least a modicum of cash for his own use, care was also taken to regulate the prices which sutlers could charge for food and drink. The following summer (1760), bakers were forbidden to take more than one penny [sterling] for baking 7lb flour into a 9lb loaf, and if payment in kind had to be made, the bakers were not to exchange 7lb bread for 7lb flour, since it was considered 'a shameful deduction from the portion allowed a soldier and too exorbitant a profit for the baker'. Shameful or not, it was evidently common practice, and James Aytoun mentions that on Dominica he and his comrades were regularly issued with 1lb bread each day in place of the regulation 1lb flour .

Comparatively generous quantities of alcohol were provided on active service, or were at the very least subsidised. Tea and coffee had yet to gain wide acceptance and water often turned out to be contaminated. Once again stoppages could be made for drinks, although regiments serving in North America in the 1760s were provided with the utensils and ingredients to brew their own spruce-beer.

There was a tendency for soldiers to dispose of what remained of their subsistence – and any other cash they had – on strong drink. The practice of distributing subsistence money on a daily basis where possible curbed any temptation to spend a whole week's subsistence in one drunken night.

Commentators both ancient and modern have tended to deplore this predilection for strong drink. While stationed at Dover Castle in 1754, Colonel James Wolfe complained: 'It has been observed that some

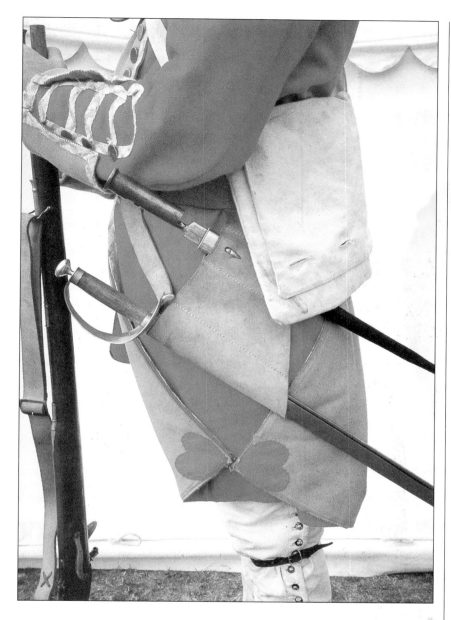

ABOVE **Reconstruction: British infantry equipment c.1745.**

soldiers go out of these barracks with a full resolution to get drunk, and have even the impudence to declare their intentions.'

# LIVING CONDITIONS

Dover Castle was in fact one of the very few barracks maintained in England during the greater part of the 18th century. At first, permanent barracks were only established where there was considered to be a pressing need to maintain a concentration of troops; for the most part they were created in existing fortresses.

### Barrack life

BELOW **Highland piper c.1743. Two pipers were normally authorised for the grenadier companies of Highland regiments in place of fifers. Unauthorised ones (including the regimental-pipe-major) also existed. [Author's collection]**

The first purpose-built barracks in England were erected at Berwick in 1721. Others were later built at Chatham, Hilsea (Portsmouth), Tynemouth, Plymouth and other locations considered worth defending. Similarly, in Scotland barrack accommodation was initially provided only in the castles at Edinburgh and Stirling. However, in the aftermath of the Jacobite Rising of 1715, a number of small barracks and police posts were erected in the Highlands, and after the last rising of 1745, a large barracks which could accommodate two battalions at once was erected at Fort George Ardersier. Ireland had large barracks at Dublin, Limerick, Kinsale, Cork, Waterford and Galway. In addition, there were a large number of smaller security posts, which often housed no more than a single company, chiefly in Ireland and Scotland.

Useful as these barracks were, they did not provide adequate accommodation for the greater part of the army. Indeed it has been estimated that by 1792 proper barrack accommodation existed for only 20,000 men, and that included the ordnance troops and invalids permanently stationed in the various forts. Consequently, most battalions serving in England, and to a lesser extent in Scotland and Ireland, had to be dispersed, often quite widely, among the civilian population in billets. Almost invariably they were accommodated in public houses or, as the annual Mutiny Acts defined them, 'inns, livery stables, alehouses, victualling houses, and all houses selling brandy, strong waters, cyder, or metheglin by retail to be drunk on the premises'.

Broadly speaking, the soldier could find himself in a purpose-built barracks or adapted mediaeval castle while serving in Scotland or England, but was more likely to be accommodated piecemeal in the loft or some other dingy corner of an inn. In Ireland his chances of living in a proper barracks were greater, but it was only really in one of the permanent foreign stations such as Gibraltar or Jamaica that he could be assured of such accommodation.

Neither barracks nor billets had anything much to commend them, for overcrowding was rife in both – even at Fort George Ardersier, which was very much a model establishment, eight men might end up sleeping two to a bed in each small barrack room. Complaints about the condition of the accommodation were also common, but for many soldiers it was a real improvement on the frequently damp and insanitary hovels in which their civilian counterparts lived.

### Married men

Soldiers were routinely discouraged from marrying but many did so, and the regulations allowed six wives per company. To be more precise, six wives and their children per company could be carried on the ration rolls and were provided with accommodation in return for hospital or other work. It is not at all clear how soldiers' wives were taken on to the strength, but it may be no coincidence that each company also had six NCOs – three sergeants and three corporals. There is no doubt that the ordinary rank and file did marry, or at least contract less formal alliances, but their position was naturally much more precarious. Regimental orderly books routinely refer to the presence of camp followers, and frequently express frustration over the difficulties of controlling them. At least official wives could be brought into line with the threat of the withdrawal of their rations and official accommodation.

Unofficial accommodation also existed. A contemporary sketch of

ABOVE **Reconstruction. Corporals were distinguished at this period by a loop of white cord, representing the extra skein of slow-match issued to corporals during the 17th century.**

Bernera Barracks in the West Highlands shows the existence of a rudimentary, but no doubt quite typical, 'married patch' comprising about a dozen 'Hutts for the Soldiers' Wives and Families'. It would be interesting to know when this sketch was made, for although the barracks was in theory capable of accommodating four companies, in practice it seems to have been occupied by only one at any one time, and in the summer of 1746 there were only ten men there, detached from the garrison at Fort William.

The only real check upon the number of women attached to an infantry battalion was the allocation of space and rations on the transports taking it to or from a foreign station. Then, and only then, could the six wives to a company rule be effectively enforced. When 1/Royals sailed for Jamaica in January 1790, for example, they embarked 349 effectives in ten companies, plus 62 women and 70 children.

It was recognised that soldiers were more likely to marry when spending long periods in garrison, and that the commonest reason for a

BELOW **'Present... fire'. Note how the soldier is taught to lean into his shot; contrast this with the much stiffer posture in the 1764 manual exercise. [Author's collection]**

ABOVE **The 'Boston Massacre' was the army's best-publicised failure in crowd control – a common enough role in England, but one which the American colonists were unused to and therefore resented.**

soldier volunteering to remain in, say, Upper Canada – either as a settler or by volunteering into another corps – was that he had a wife who could not be accommodated on the transport taking the battalion home.

## CAREER

With our recruit now paid, fed, clothed and given some kind of a roof over his head, we can examine the likely course of his career. Although he started off by enlisting in a particular regiment, there was no guarantee that he would remain with it for very long; there was every chance that by the time he was discharged he would have passed through a number of different units. James Aytoun originally enlisted in the 58th Foot, in January 1786, but in August of the following year he volunteered to transfer into the 9th Foot, which was under orders for service in the

ABOVE **Leather flap covering belly-box – bearing an unusual George II cypher.** [Author's collection]

West Indies. No sooner had he arrived in Barbados, in April 1788, than he was drafted straight into the 30th Foot. The drafting of men from one unit to another was commonplace in the 18th century. It was most common when a unit – particularly one from the weak Irish establishment – was ordered overseas and had to be brought up to its authorised strength in a hurry. Often the only practical way in which to accomplish this was to strip men from other units. Conversely when an understrength unit was ordered home to recruit, its existing rank and file would first be drafted into units remaining in theatre.

New regiments were also cause for drafting. At the outset, wherever possible, men were drafted into the unit from older corps in order to form a disciplined cadre around which the new regiment could be formed. But no sooner would it be brought up to strength than the newly trained recruits would be drafted to fill out other, longer-established, regiments. Finally, if a regiment was disbanded at the end of the war which had called it into existence, its remaining personnel, although entitled to their discharge on the spot, would normally find themselves offered fresh bounties to re-enlist in regiments expected to survive.

Whichever regiment he joined or at least ended up in, our recruit first had to undergo basic training. He had to learn how to carry himself, to march in step, and all the other little things that would enable him to fit into military life. Ideally, training would take place at one of the big depots such as Chatham or Kinsale, but in practice the high turnover of recruits and wide dispersion of quarters usually meant that it would not happen until he joined his company. The amount of training he actually received before finding himself on the battlefield would vary, but it seems to have been generally agreed that it took about a year to turn a recruit into an efficient soldier.

Once he was properly trained, a soldier might remain with one of the eight battalion companies or be posted to a flank company. Prior to 1771, each infantry battalion had a grenadier company. In 1771, a light infantry company was added. Traditionally, grenadiers were drawn from the tallest and strongest men in the battalion, but this practice seems to have been the case only when a regiment was formed from scratch. In well-established corps, it was more usual to fill the ranks of the grenadier company with the steadier and more mature men – those who could be depended upon in a crisis, irrespective of their height. Similarly, the light company, although requiring nimble, active men, clearly also required good soldiers with stamina and more intelligence than might have been expected from the raw farm boys newly swept up by recruiters. Indeed, there are indications that, in some units at least, a good soldier would expect to be posted first to the light company and then, as his breath failed him, on to the grenadiers.

LEFT **Reconstruction: Goatskin knapsack c.1760 onwards.**

LEFT **Reconstruction: Reverse side of knapsack showing arrangement of straps. The shoulder straps are anchored top and bottom so that all adjustment is by means of the breast strap.**

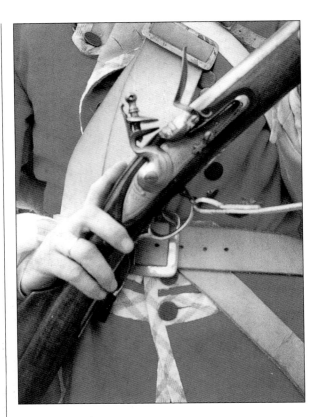

ABOVE **Short land pattern firelock: lock detail – flash pan open. [Author's collection]**

## Promotion

Although a posting to either a grenadier or a light company meant an increase in status – and probably a corresponding increase in net subsistence money with which he might be entitledx– the first upward step by way of promotion was to the rank of corporal. This brought a modest increase in pay and probably a rather greater increase in responsibility (although he would still shoulder a firelock and stand in the ranks).

After that, if he was fit for it, he could be promoted to sergeant. This was a far more responsible post. Apart from anything else, it required, in practice, the ability to read and write. Normally this was the pinnacle of a recruit's career (sergeant-major and quartermaster-sergeant were appointments at this period rather than ranks). However, for a fortunate few it was possible to go further and be commissioned – to become an officer.

Despite the domination of the purchase system, promotion of rankers to a commissioned rank was surprisingly common in the 18th-century British army – perhaps more so than in the 19th century, when a distinct officer caste began to emerge.

## Rising from the ranks

Promoted rankers generally fell into one of three categories: the old and steady, the exceptionally brave, and the volunteers. The first category was perhaps the largest, and included commissioned quartermasters; by the end of the 18th century, it was a rank invariably drawn from experienced quartermaster-sergeants. Particularly able sergeants were also promoted to fill company vacancies. This happened chiefly in newly raised regiments where their experience and talents were at a premium, although inspection returns reveal that most regiments usually had at least one former ranker amongst their subalterns. Obviously such experience was not gained overnight, and the four sergeants commissioned into the newly raised 64th Foot in 1756 had between 12 and 22 years' service in the ranks behind them. These comparatively old officers often found it difficult to rise much further, although it was not unknown: George Edington was promoted to sergeant in 1/Royals on 30 December 1790 and was commissioned just three and a half years later. By 6 December 1798 he was a captain.

Promotion of the exceptionally brave was much more haphazard. Where a man's character or ability was not considered equal to his bravery, he might be commissioned into an invalid company or some other obscure billet, rather than his own corps. In such a case, promotion was obviously a dead end, although the eventual prospect of the half-pay this offered was not lightly disregarded. For others, however, a promotion of this nature could once again be a stepping stone to better things. Sergeant Terry Molloy, described by General Sir John Cope in 1745 as 'a verie good sergeant', received a lieutenant's commission after he and a dozen men successfully defended Ruthven Barracks against three hundred Jacobite rebels. Ten years later, further promotion came after he successfully fought his way out of Braddock's disaster on the Monongahela river.

The third category, the 'volunteers', were for the most part men who lacked the money and influence necessary to obtain a commission by more conventional means; they enlisted to serve in the ranks in the hope of one day being offered any vacancy which arose. Naturally such opportunities occurred most frequently in wartime or when a battalion was far from home. On active service there were obvious advantages for all concerned, in that the vacancy could be filled on the spot instead of waiting for a replacement to be sent from home. At the same time, the volunteer, by virtue of having served for a time in the ranks, would come to the job with some useful training and experience. Just as importantly, perhaps, he would have gained an empathy with the rank and file which a newly hatched ensign commissioned straight from school would never attain.

Just how widespread the practice of promoting volunteers was is hard to assess, since it is often unclear whether the local promotions recorded in orderly books refer to volunteers or deserving NCOs.

Samuel Bagshawe enlisted as a private in the 26th Foot in 1731 and served seven years in the Gibraltar garrison, eventually becoming quartermaster sergeant. For an Englishman serving in a Scottish regiment this was considered to be pretty good going at the time. He only escaped from the ranks when his uncle bought him out, and two years later he obtained an ensign's commission in the 30th Foot through the influence of the Duke of Devonshire. More typical, perhaps, was a 19-year-old Inverness-shire man, John Urquhart. The son of a grenadier wounded at Belle Isle in 1761, he served two years in the ranks of 1/Royals before obtaining an ensign's commission without purchase in January 1791 and ultimately working up to Captain. (See MAA 285 *King George's Army 1740-93 Vol.1*).

Oddly enough, in the summer of 1794 no fewer than three out of the 11 officers actually on duty in 1/Royals had begun their career in the ranks. Odder still, they also represented the three main strands by which rankers could gain promotion: Urquhart, of course, was a volunteer; George Edington had gained his commission through merit and perhaps a bit of conspicuous bravery, since promotion from Sergeant came in the wake of the capture of Port au Prince; and the eldest of the trio, Alexander Davidson, had accelerated up from quartermaster

ABOVE **Short land pattern firelock: displaying the characteristic 'tailed' brass sideplate.**

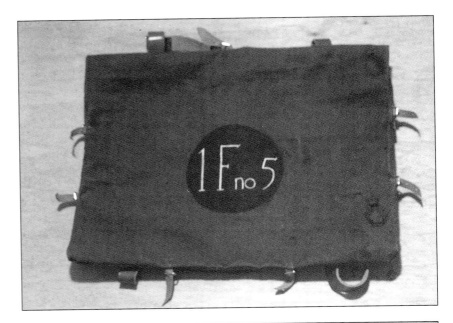

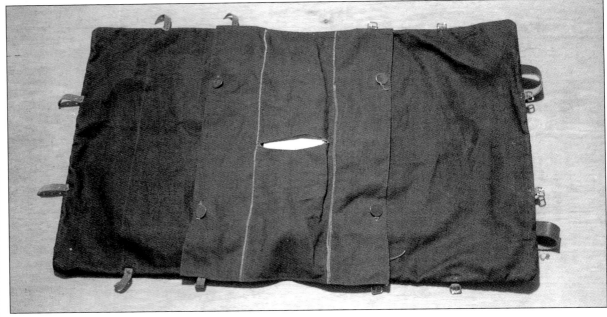

ABOVE **Reconstruction: Interior of folding knapsack showing its three compartments. Modern folding luggage is made to virtually the same pattern.**

sergeant to quartermaster and then to an ensign's commission, dying shortly before his promotion to Lieutenant was approved.

### Discharge from the army

Leaving the army was in some ways surprisingly easy. Conscripts such as the vestry men who earned the army such an ugly reputation after Culloden were enlisted for six months or until the end of the emergency. The volunteers who joined the dozen or so provincial regiments raised at the same time were also discharged when the fighting was over, but each was given a small gratuity of six days' pay if he elected to go home, or a bounty of two guineas if he re-enlisted in a regular unit. Similarly, during the American War of Independence, a dearth of recruits led to the temporary introduction of short engagements – three years or till the end of the war.

Otherwise, accepting the 'King's shilling' meant, in theory, entering His Majesty's service for life. In practice this was rarely the case, except where the soldier died of wounds or disease. Normally a soldier, if wishing to leave the army for whatever reason, could obtain his discharge in a number of ways.

In the first place, if a soldier was promoted to commissioned rank, he was first discharged from the rolls of his regiment. If a unit was disbanded at the end of a war, all its NCOs and rank and file were also entitled to receive their discharge. Furthermore, prior to 1770, battalions carried on the Irish establishment mustered only half the number of rank and file allowed to battalions on the British establishment. Consequently those men surplus to requirements when a battalion was transferred to the Irish establishment had to be discharged. There was, of course, a fair chance that any discharged soldier might immediately be picked up by a recruiting party for another unit, but there was no obligation on him to re-enlist.

Similarly, when a unit was ordered home from a colonial posting, soldiers could elect either to be drafted into a unit remaining in the country or, if their own regiment was going home to be disbanded, they could obtain their discharge as free settlers and receive a land-grant into the bargain.

### Benefits and pensions

Soldiers wounded in battle or crippled by disease in the King's service – venereal diseases and chronic alcoholism did not count – were entitled to a range of benefits according to their circumstances.

For the worst cases, there were a limited number of places in the Royal Hospitals at Chelsea and Kilmainham for the British and Irish establishments respectively. Oddly enough, a soldier's entitlement to a place, or to a pension from either establishment, depended upon which establishment his regiment was carried by at the time of his discharge. So soldiers originally enlisted in Scotland for, say, the 105th Highlanders could find themselves granted a place or a pension from Kilmainham since their regiment was serving on the Irish establishment at the time of its disbandment.

Any soldier still capable of loading his firelock might be assigned to one of the regiments or independent companies of invalids employed in garrison duties. Such units normally served as little more than night-watchmen at military installations in the British Isles, but during the Seven Years War, a battalion was organised to look after the British base at Bremen. Another served in North America in the 1770s. Although these invalids could occasionally be called upon to fight, or help control rioting, their function was more charitable than military.

Entitlement to a pension was limited during this period to those who were in some measure disabled in the service. In other words, if a man was discharged fit and healthy, there was considered to be no reason why he should not be able to support himself, and the best he could reasonably hope for was a gratuity of a few days' subsistence, sufficient to carry him to his home parish. If, on the other hand, he had been wounded or otherwise disabled in the service, he could be granted an 'out-pension' from either Chelsea of Kilmainham. Prior to the 1750s, long service was not in itself a qualification for a pension, but it is clear from the registers that in practice old soldiers could receive one after being certified as 'worn out'.

# TRAINING AND TACTICS

On joining his regiment, the recruit was issued with a basic suit of clothing and embarked upon basic training. Writing in 1759, William Windham prefaced the second part of his excellent *Plan of Discipline for the Use of the Norfolk Militia* with the following remarks: 'We must, in the first place, recommend to all gentlemen, who intend to act as militia officers, to arm themselves with a great deal of patience, as they must expect to find many of the countrymen infinitely awkward and stiff; especially those who are turned thirty years of age, and have been used to hard labour. These (though willing and attentive) cannot easily bring their limbs to execute what they are taught, although they perfectly comprehend it. In others they will find a great want of apprehension and memory, and an amazing difficulty of understanding and retain[ing] things and ideas that are new to them, and different from what they have been used to from their cradle. Others again are lazy, careless and want attention. These are certainly very disagreeable circumstances, and must often put an officer's temper to hard trials.'

First the recruit was taught to be the 'master of his person', that is to carry himself properly – 'chin up, shoulders back and stomach in'. Having thus started off the process of smartening himself up, he proceeded to learn the intricacies of foot drill and maintaining his dressing while marching. The latter was particularly important, for while it was certainly required that he should set off with the left foot, before the 1750s he was not actually required to march in step except when carrying out what were quaintly termed 'evolutions' – changes of front or formation. Consequently, dressing had to be preserved by maintaining physical contact with the man next to him while marching.

### Weapons training

Once he had mastered, or at least proved himself to be reasonably proficient in, foot drill and marching, he was finally introduced to his firelock. As today, the very first lesson was the naming of the parts. That done, he then learned the 'manual exercise' or weapon handling – first without ammunition, then with blank charges and finally with ball.

Of necessity this was a slow process, with the same one-two timing between each movement as is practised today. Once it had been mastered, he moved on to learn the platoon exercise or, more precisely, to learning and practising the actions required of him. This basically entailed getting used to loading and firing in three ranks, which in turn involved not only weapon handling, but endless practice in locking – an important drill movement which is discussed in greater detail below.

Firing at a mark was generally held to be a good thing by everybody except the Treasury. The allocation varied throughout the period, but in peacetime, battalions normally received sufficient powder for between

31,000 and 60,000 rounds a year. If a battalion was fully up to its authorised Establishment, this should have allowed something in the region of 60 to 120 rounds per man; in practice, the allocation was slightly higher, since few battalions were ever fully recruited.

This allocation was probably sufficient to practice the firings as a drill. However, until 1785, battalions also received only a niggardly one hundredweight of shot per annum – roughly 1,200 rounds of ball. The two to four rounds of ball each man could expect to fire in a year would barely have been enough to accustom him to the greater kick of firing a fully loaded weapon, let alone gain any skill in marksmanship. It is little wonder then that in 1774 Major General William Howe reported that the 3rd Foot 'have not fired Ball for some years'. The previous year, Major General Alexander Mackay had returned from a busy summer's reviews to report: 'The Powder given to the Troops is in General very bad, the Flints remarkably so; And the Quantity of Ball so small, that it is impossible to practice the men to fire at Marks, as should be done constantly.'

Rather belatedly, in 1786, the peacetime allocation of ball ammunition to each battalion was upped to 9,600 rounds a year, which then worked out at about 30 rounds per man. This was still on the low side, but a considerable improvement nonetheless. In any case, it was a different matter in wartime, with ball ammunition then available on demand, and most regiments threw themselves into firing it off with considerable enthusiasm. In the summer of 1757 the 15th Foot were reported to be out three days a week firing seven rounds of ball per man: 'Every man has fired about 84 rounds, and now load and fire Ball with as much coolness and allacrity in all the different fireings as ever you saw them fire blank powder, hitherto without the smallest accident,' it was reported.

Similarly, the order book of Captain James Stewart's company of the 42nd Highlanders reveals the light company firing at marks on 10 March 1759. The whole battalion was out for three successive days at the beginning of April. (The entry for 4 April 1759 usefully directs: 'All the shooting boards to be covered with papper and a black spot in the middle'.) After that promising start, however, all the ball ammunition was withdrawn to ensure that there were no accidents at a forthcoming review, prior to their marching off to war. As a further precaution, it was prudently arranged that all the 'awkward men' in the battalion would be posted on guard that day, safely out of view of the inspecting officer.

There is little doubt that the soldiers themselves were aware of the importance of good shooting, and Stewart's order book contains a number of references to the prevalence of soldiers going out and shooting up farmers' fences and other informal 'marks'. Poaching was also rife.

Notwithstanding such official and unofficial practice, the common firelock was not a particularly accurate weapon beyond about 50 metres, so tactical doctrines were framed to compensate for this: lay down as heavy a fire as possible at close range.

### Fighting tactics

For much of the period, infantry fighting doctrines were governed, or at least heavily influenced, by the 1728 Regulations, which had in turn been cribbed from Humphrey Bland's elegantly written *Treatise of Military Discipline*, first published in 1727. The importance of Bland's drill-book may be gauged by the fact that it went through no fewer than nine editions, the last being published in 1762.

According to Bland's system, the battalion was divided into four grand divisions for the purposes of manoeuvre, and a much larger number of platoons for fire-control purposes. In the forming of these divisions and platoons (the two bore little or no relationship to each other), the various companies were divided up as required and only the grenadiers survived as an independent unit. The following extracts from Bland provide a useful and very clear insight into how a battalion was actually supposed to work on the battlefield:

### Bland's system of military discipline

In the Drawing up of a Battalion for Exercise, or a Review, the Ranks are to be at four ordinary Paces Distance from one another.

When they are to fire, either by Ranks, Platoons, the whole Battalion, or in the Square, the Ranks are to be moved up to half Distance, which is two Paces.

In all Wheelings, either by Division or the whole Battalion, the Ranks are to be closed forward to close Order, which is one Pace Distance.

When a Regiment is to exercise, or to be reviewed, the Files are to be opened, the Distance of which between one and another, is one Pace, or the Length of an out-stretch'd Arm; but that this may appear more plain, as soon as the Files are open'd, and the Men faced to their proper Front, order those of the Front-rank to stretch out their Right Arms to the Right, and if they can touch the left Shoulders of their Right hand Men, they have their true Distance; the doing of which now and then, will give them a just Notion of the proper Distance. As the men of the Rear-ranks are to be governed by, and dress with those in the Front, who are called their File leaders, there is no occasion for their doing it.

When they are to fire, the Files are to be at half a Pace Distance, that the Men may have room to handle their Arms in firing and loading; which Distance is the Half of an out-stretch'd Arm; that is, when the Hand is set bent against the Side, the Elbow is to touch the Right-hand Man.

In Marching or Wheeling, the Files must be so close, that the Men almost touch one another with their Shoulders.'

So far so good, but exercising proper fire-control was a little more difficult: 'The Company of Granadiers is to be divided into two Platoons, the Captain and second Lieutenant placing themselves at the Head of that on the Right and the first Lieutenant on that on the Left. One Serjeant and one Drummer are to remain with the right Platoon, the other two Serjeants and Drummer are to march with the left Platoon.

When the Company of Granadiers is thus divided, and the Officers, Serjeants, and Drummers, have posted themselves on the Right and Left Platoons, according to the above Directions, they are to face to the Left on their right Heels, and to march to the Left beginning with the Feet they faced on. The first Lieutenant with his Platoon of Granadiers is to march along the Ranks of the Battalion until the Right-hand File of his Platoon has got one Pace beyond the Left-hand File of the Battalion, and then halt, and make them dress with the Battalion. As soon as the Left-hand File of the Right Platoon of Granadiers comes within a Pace of the Right-hand File of the Battalion, the Captain is to order them to halt, and make them dress with the others.

The Major is to order the Men to fix their Bayonets, it being the custom to perform the Firings with the Bayonets fix'd on the Muzzle; which, however, may be omitted in common Exercise, if the Commanding Officer thinks proper; but never on Service.

When the Bayonets are fixed, the Battalion is to be divided into Platoons; the Number of which must depend upon the strength of the Battalion, and the particular Firings you intend to perform. Neither is a Platoon composed of any fixed number of Files but may be more or less, according as the Battalion will allow of it; However a Platoon is seldom composed of less than 10 Files, which are 30 Men, or more than 16 Files, which are 48 Men; because a Platoon composed of less than 10 Files would not be of Weight enough to do any considerable Execution; and those above 16 Files would be too great a Body of Men for an Officer to manage upon Service.

In dividing the Battalion into Platoons, they should be composed of an equal number of Files; or at least not above one File stronger than another, and those should be the Flanks and Colour [centre] Platoons.

As soon as the Platoons are told off, there must be an Officer appointed to each, to command them; taking an equal proportion of Captains, Lieutenant and Ensigns for that Purpose.

The Lieutenant Colonel, with the remaining part of the Officers, are to march, and post themselves in the Rear of the Battalion in the same Manner as they do at Exercise, the Captains, Lieutenant and Ensigns drawing up into one Rank in the rear of the Serjeants, and the Lieutenant Colonel in the Rear of the Officers, and opposite to the Colour Platoon.

BELOW **The Retreat from Concord: This action is widely held to illustrate how ill-equipped the British army was to deal with light troops, but in the circumstances Colonel Smith and his men did remarkably well. [Author's collection]**

The Serjeants should be divided to the several Platoons, and posted in the Rear of them.

The Colonel, and the Ensigns with the Colours, remain in the former Posts at the Head of the Battalion.

The Reasons for the Officers being posted in the Rear, are as follows: First, As the Interval between each Platoon should be but one Pace, the Officer who commands the Platoon is to fall into it when they fire; therefore, should any more Officers remain in the Front, than one to each Platoon, it would only embarrass and expose them to their own Fire.

Secondly. It is of great Use to have experienced Officers in the Rear, to keep the Men up, and see that they do their Duty in Action; as also to lead the Battalion off in Order, when they are commanded to retire; for which reason they place a Proportion of each Rank there. And lastly, should there be no officers in the Rear when the Battalion is ordered to the Right about, the Men would be apt to march off too fast, and by that Means break their Ranks, and fall into Confusion, or not halt in due Time; which inconveniences are prevented by Officers being posted there.

### Firing by platoon

The Method which is now practis'd, and which by Experience, is found to be the most useful, is, the dividing of the Platoons into several Firings; each Firing being seldom composed of less than four Platoons, or more than five; which Firings are not kept together in any one part of the Battalion; but the Platoons of each Firing distributed, or disposed into different parts of the Regiment; the Reasons for disposing of them into different Parts, are these:

First. The Disposing of the Platoons of each Firing into different Parts of the Battalion, will extend your Fire in such a Manner, as to do great Execution in different Parts of the opposite Regiment; the Consequence of which, may either disable or dishearten them so much, as, upon a nearer Approach, to oblige them to give Way, or make but a faint Resistance.

Secondly. Their being divided in this Manner, should the Enemy and you join before those Platoons have Time to load, not any one Part of your Battalion is very much weakened by it; however, when the Commanding Officer apprehends that this may be the Case, he must avoid it, by leaving off after the first or second Firings, that they may all be loaded by the Time they join the Enemy in order to throw in their Whole upon them at once.

Thirdly. Should the Platoons of each Firing be together, too great a Part of the Battalion would be exposed in one Place before the men could load, particularly the Flank Firings.

Fourthly, and lastly. The Firings being thus disposed of, it makes the Exercise appear the more beautiful, and accustoms the Men to hear Firing on their Right and Left, without touching their Arms till they have Orders for it, which the English are with Difficulty brought to, from a natural Desire and Eagerness to enter soon into Action; a Quality in some cases extremely commendable, but in others the contrary; for which Reason the Men must be taught to rely entirely on the Conduct of their Officers; and to wait with Patience for their Orders, before they perform any Motion; the due Performance of which, both their Safety and Honour depend upon.'

## Drawbacks in the firing system

There was a problem with the famous platoon firing system which Bland rather softly hints at: it was over-complicated and sometimes did not work.

There were essentially two reasons for this. First, by dividing a battalion up into evenly sized platoons, the normal company-based command structure was necessarily disrupted. It is perhaps too easy to overestimate the effects of this, since proper training – or, more accurately, rehearsal – should have overcome the worst of them. The second – and real – reason why the platoon firing system tended to break down was that all too often such training and rehearsal was lacking. This, in turn, can be attributed to a number of factors, chiefly that it was rarely possible to assemble enough officers and men in one place at one time to practise platooning properly. Except for the footguards, concentrated in London and near to Hyde Park, and the regiments of the Dublin garrison, close to Phoenix Park, most units were too widely scattered to carry out the necessary training.

Considerable time was also spent on providing aid to the civil authorities, road-making in Scotland and simply on marching from one quarter to another. Obviously, it was possible to carry out a certain amount of training on a daily basis, even if it were restricted to the manual exercise (weapon handling) and basic foot drill, but except in the weeks immediately preceding an annual inspection it appears to have been rare for a regiment of the line to have been able to practise platooning.

The result, perhaps predictably, was an utter shambles when the British army had its first real opportunity to put Bland's teaching into practice, at Dettingen in 1743. Far from being carefully controlled, the firing was generally agreed to have been wild and undisciplined. James Wolfe, then the adjutant of the 12th Foot, wrote that he had spent the day 'begging and ordering the men not to fire at too great a distance... but to little purpose. The whole fired when they thought they could reach them, which had like to have ruined us. We did very little execution with it'.

Perhaps not surprisingly in the circumstances, he was also later moved to write: 'I have a very mean opinion of the infantry in general. I know their discipline to be bad, & their valour precarious. They are easily put into disorder, & hard to recover out of it; they frequently kill their Officers thro' fear, & murder one another in their confusion.'

## Improvement in tactics

Perhaps the only consolation was that the French had proved to be even worse in discipline. Afterwards an intensive training programme was embarked upon, which reaped its rewards at Fontenoy and Culloden. It is no coincidence that Cope's army, routed so spectacularly at Prestonpans, was made up of untried regiments which had only been concentrated for the first time a month before, and that Cumberland's victorious army at Culloden preceded its final advance to contact with six weeks of rigorous training in its cantonments around Aberdeen.

Notwithstanding the improvements bought by proper training, it was still generally recognised that Bland's platooning was too complicated, and a number of units soon experimented with and developed 'improvements'. These were vigorously discouraged by the Duke of Cumberland, who had no wish to see the hard-won efficiency of his regiments destroyed by the abandonment of a common drill-book. Nevertheless, some useful refinements were authorised in 1748 and again in 1756/7.

Doubtless drawing upon wartime experience, the 1748 Regulations simplified Bland's platoon exercise by leaving off a reserve, reducing the number of firings to three and, perhaps more significantly, by formally linking platoons and grand divisions. Under the 1748 Regulations, there were now to be four platoons in each of the four grand divisions.

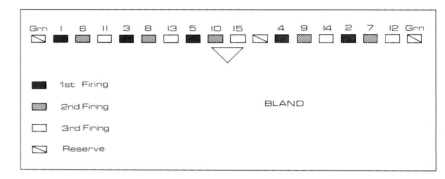

RIGHT **Platoon firing sequence as recommended by Humphrey Bland in 1727. According to circumstances and regimental practice, all the platoons in each 'firing' could deliver their volleys together, or else each platoon could fire individually, according to the pre-arranged numerical sequence. [Author's collection]**

The 1756/7 Regulations essentially retained the simplified platooning of the 1748 Regulations but took a major step forward in closing up the distances between files. Bland, as we have seen, advocated an interval of half a pace between each file, or in effect a frontage of about 30in (0.75m) per man when firing. The 1756 Regulations closed this frontage up to 24in (0.6m) per man.

At the same time, close order (one pace of about 30in) became pretty much the standard distance between ranks for firing as well as manoeuvring. This speeded up the locking of ranks and hence the rate of fire. In the early days when three ranks fired at once, the front rank went down on one knee, the second crouched a little and only the rear rank remained upright. This created two problems: first, if the centre rank did not crouch low enough, it was difficult for the rear rank to do other than fire in the air; secondly, the distance between ranks placed

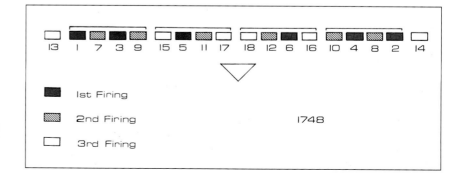

RIGHT **The slightly simpler platoon firing sequence established in the 1748 Regulations. Note how there should ideally be four platoons in each of the four 'grand divisions'. [Author's collection]**

the muzzles of the rear rank firelocks uncomfortably close to the heads of the men in the front rank. Bland's drill-book solved this problem by advocating the locking of ranks immediately before firing.

All the loading and reloading was done at the proper intervals. When ordered to 'lock', the front rank went down on one knee as before, but otherwise did not move. The centre rank closed up hard on the first and took half a pace to the right, while the third rank similarly stepped forward and took a full pace to the right. By this means the file was now ranged in echelon with the centre man firing down the gap between the front rank man and his neighbour on the right. The rear rank man was firing over the head of that neighbour, but was sufficiently close to him to obviate any danger of blowing his head off.

Notwithstanding these improvements, the 1748 and 1756/7 Regulations essentially did little more than tinker with Bland's system. In the meantime a number of regiments were engaged in the quite unauthorised development of the 'alternate' system of firing, which would eventually replace Bland's platooning in the 1764 Regulations.

By comparison with Bland's platooning, the alternate system was simplicity itself. Proceeding on active service, a battalion would first equalise its companies – that is, transfer men from one to another until they were all roughly the same size. Each company then acted as a platoon, commanded in action by its own officers. As a further refinement, the eight battalion companies (the Establishment was reduced from nine to eight at the end of the Seven Years War) were also paired off to form the subdivisions of the four grand divisions required for manoeuvring.

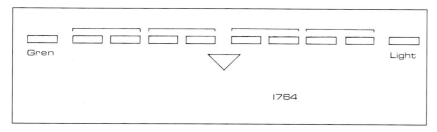

LEFT **The final version of platoon firing as laid down in 1764. Battalion companies are paired off to form the four grand divisions. Each company also fires as one platoon under the control of its own officers. [Author's collection]**

The sequence of firing was also considerably simplified. The platoons prescribed by Bland, and the later 1748 Regulations, were numbered off both as to the three or four firings and in a straightforward numerical sequence so that volleys could be delivered in one of two ways. Either all the platoons of the first firing could blaze away at once and at the same time, followed by the platoons of the second firing and so on, or each individual platoon could fire one after the other according to their numerical sequence.

This may well have looked fine at Hyde Park or Phoenix Park, but as Major George Grant remarked in 1757: 'I deny regular Platooning being Battle Form, it is too formal for that, and never done without some Mistakes. Why should a Platoon stay four or five Minutes waiting for Regularity? perhaps all knocked on the Head before it came to their Turn to fire again. . . no Commander to stay a Moment after his Platoon is loaded, but Present and Fire immediately, until the Number of Rounds are gone that is allowed him for that Manner of Fireing. Then will you see right Battle Form. Why should we train Men up in one

Method, and leave them to find out another how to fight the Enemy. For these regular Platooners, as soon as you take them out of the Way they are taught, will be all in confusion.'

Grant, admittedly, had seen no active service since being cashiered for a too hasty surrender of Fort George, Inverness, in 1746, but it is hard to deny the force of his argument, and the much simpler firing sequences of the 1764 Regulations were undoubtedly a great improvement.

There still remained a danger, as at Dettingen, that the longer firing went on the more likely it was that platoons would begin firing out of sequence and that ultimately the firefight might degenerate into each individual soldier loading and firing as fast as he could. However, close attention paid to the manual exercise led to the average British soldier being able to load and fire his weapon faster than his continental counterpart. This, rather than the overrated platoon firing system taught by Bland, may in part explain the noted British superiority in firing.

## Grenadier and light infantry units

It would still have been necessary to exert a measure of control over the firing, and in reviews it was customary to limit any particular phase of firing to a stated number of rounds. There seems no reason to doubt that the same method of control was exercised in combat – as indeed Major Grant recommends.

Common to both platoon and alternate firing was the practice of treating the grenadier company as an entirely separate unit. This was done for two reasons. In the first place, it was sometimes helpful to have a reserve of experienced men specifically charged with guarding the battalion's flanks in battle. Secondly, it became increasingly common for the grenadier company to be detached from its parent unit.

The grenadier's role in the 18th century was an interesting one. Grenade throwing had from the beginning been only incidental to their real role as fast moving assault troops. It was a role which they retained, despite the effective abandonment of the hand grenade, which was only of any real use in assaulting or defending fortifications. Indeed, under the alternate fire system, the grenadiers were soon paired off with the newly introduced light company. When a battalion was drawn up as a single organic unit, the grenadiers would often be tasked with skirmishing on the right of the battalion, while the light company skirmished on the left.

It became increasingly common, however, for both flank companies to be drawn off from their parent units and formed with other similar companies into provisional assault battalions. Although the practice seems to have been pioneered during the Seven Years War, both in Germany and in North America, the most notable example of it was to be seen during the American War of Independence. All the grenadier companies serving in that theatre were formed into four semi-permanent battalions of grenadiers, and the light companies into four light infantry battalions. These provisional units appear to have built up a considerable *esprit de corps*, and within a short time their officers, and presumably by extension their men, were taking to describing themselves as serving in the British Grenadiers rather than belonging to their parent battalions.

The extent to which their roles differed is difficult to gauge, since both grenadiers and light infantry were expected to serve either as skirmishers or as shock troops as the occasion demanded. Indeed, where it was impractical to form separate battalions of grenadiers and light infantry, as on San Domingo in 1794, a single composite 'flank battalion' would be formed from grenadier and light companies. This linkage may at first appear surprising, but it was entirely in accordance with Continental thinking on the employment of light troops.

In North America, the locally raised ranger companies were supplemented by the formation of a light infantry company in each regular battalion. These companies and the 80th Light Infantry who followed were tasked with scouting and skirmishing in the woods. At pretty much the same time in Europe, however, volunteers were also being taken from the British regiments serving in Germany to form a battalion of chasseurs under a Major Fraser. As in America, a number of light infantry - or rather 'light armed' regiments - were soon raised. These included a number of Highland regiments, who are frequently described as being among the earliest light infantry units in the British army. In a sense, this is true, although it would be quite wrong to regard them as skirmishers.

Those who saw action were shipped overseas as quickly as they were raised, without proper training in the platoon exercise or much else in the way of drill. Their role, however, was not to stand shoulder to shoulder in the line of battle or to skirmish from behind cover, but to serve as lightly equipped formations capable of undertaking rapid marches and heavy raids deep into enemy territory. Once in contact with the enemy, they almost invariably went straight in with the bayonet. In effect, their role was not unlike that of the modern air-mobile brigade.

At the end of the Seven Years War, both the regimental light companies and the light infantry regiments were disbanded. (It was a common misconception, both in Britain and on the Continent, that all light troops were a rascally set of banditti who were of some use in wartime, but had no role to play in a peacetime army.)

Sufficient interest remained to see the official formation of light companies in all regiments on the British Establishment in 1771 and in the Irish Establishment in 1772. It was one thing to order that these light companies be formed; quite another to produce a competent body of light infantry. So in 1774 Major General William Howe, who had gained some very useful experience of light infantry work in North America, devised a 'discipline' for the new companies and managed to exercise some of them in it just before the outbreak of the American War of Independence. This 'discipline' was in some respects rather limited. Although marksmanship was stressed, together with considerable practice in 'irregular & bush fighting', the real meat of the training was to enable them to manoeuvre - and fire - in accordance with the 1764 Regulations while dispersed in open, or even extended, order.

### Evolution of light infantry tactics

Once appointed commander-in-chief in North America, Howe then took the whole process a stage further by effectively training all his regular infantry as light troops. In the 1750s, the intervals between ranks and files had been tightened up quite considerably in order to speed up

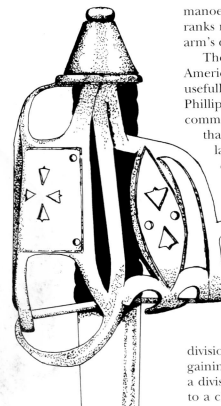

manoeuvring. But Howe trained his battalions to march and fight in two ranks rather than three - and to do it in open order, that is, with a full arm's distance between each file.

The result may not have been very pretty, but this 'loose file and American scramble' served the army well throughout the war, and is usefully described in a set of standing orders issued by Major General Phillips: 'It is the Major General's wish, that the troops under his command may practice forming from two to three and four deep; and that they should be accustomed to charge in all those orders. In the latter orders, of the three and four deep, the files will, in course, be closer, so as to render a charge of the greatest force. The Major General also recommends to regiments the practice of dividing the battalions, by wings or otherwise, so that one line may support the other when an attack is supposed; and, when a retreat is supposed, that the first line may retreat through the intervals of the second, the second doubling up its divisions for that purpose, and forming again in order to check the enemy who may be supposed to have pressed the first line. The Major General would approve also of one division of a battalion attacking in the common open order of two deep, to be supported by the other compact division as a second line, in a charging order of three or four deep. The gaining the flanks also of a supposed enemy, by the quick movements of a division in common open order, while the compact division advances to a charge; and such other evolutions, as may lead the regiments to a custom of depending on and mutually supporting each other; so that should one part be pressed or broken, it may be accustomed to form again without confusion, under the protection of a second line, or any regular formed division.'

From this and from other similar descriptions, it is clear that the tactics employed by the British army during the American War of Independence were radically different from those practised in Europe. Gone was the solid firing line; instead there were, to all intents and purposes, a heavy screen of light infantry backed up by solider assault columns ready to exploit any weakness in the enemy lines. The frequency with which 'charging' (presumably with the bayonet) was stressed is also significant.

The troops ranged in these loose files were not intended to act as skirmishers per se; although the regimental light companies (and to a certain extent the grenadiers as well) were trained in that role, particularly in broken ground, it generally remained the prerogative of specialist units of riflemen and marksmen.

In the light of this distinction between light troops and skirmishers it is perhaps less surprising to find so much reliance still placed upon the bayonet, despite the fact that Culloden, in 1746, was apparently the only occasion on which it was wielded in earnest. The bayonet used throughout the period was a 17in fluted iron spike with a wickedly sharp

ABOVE **Munition quality broadsword hilt as issued to the rank and file of Highland regiments. [Author's collection]**

BELOW **Typical Land Pattern bayonet as made by John Gill of Birmingham. [Author's collection]**

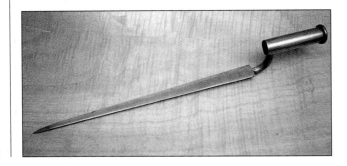

Private, 8th (King's) Regiment, 1748 (See text commentary for detailed captions)

**B**

Recruiting for the 80th Foot, 1780

Recruits drilling at Chatham, 1791

**D**

43rd Highlanders on the march, 1743

**Head-dress (See text commentary for detailed captions)**

E

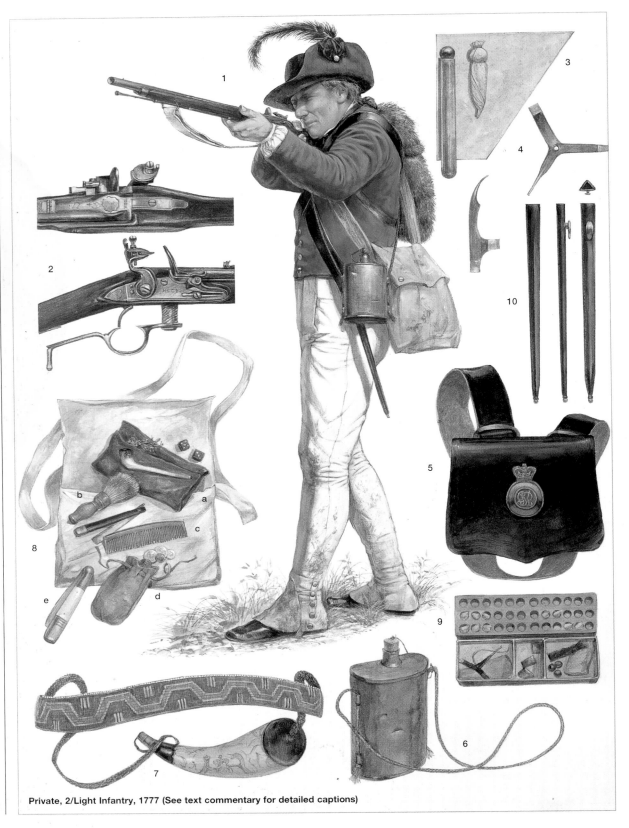

F

Private, 2/Light Infantry, 1777 (See text commentary for detailed captions)

Skirmish at Zierenberg, 1760

**H**

37th Foot at Battle of Culloden, 1746

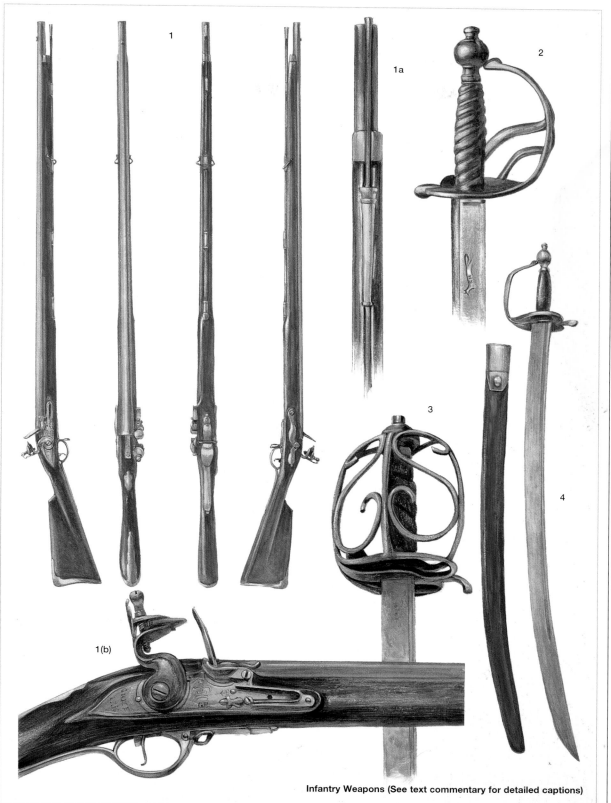

**Infantry Weapons (See text commentary for detailed captions)**

After the Battle, Guilford Courthouse, 1781

21st Foot encamped, Roermond, Holland, 1748

**K**

Private, 1/Royals, 1789 (See text commentary for detailed captions)

L

point . Although it also made a surprisingly handy dagger, its real function was to intimidate rather than to kill or wound. This is particularly obvious if you study the rather limited training given in its use. Bland outlines what is, to all intents and purposes, the old pike drill practised during the English Civil War. The soldier stands at right angles to his front with the firelock and bayonet levelled across his chest, shoulder high, with the right hand grasping the butt. On the word of command 'push', he was expected to do just that, driving it forward with the right hand.

This surprisingly stiff technique worked well enough at Culloden. Perhaps as a result, it survived through the 1748 and 1756/7 Regulations. However, Windham's privately published Norfolk Discipline of 1759 argued vigorously against it: 'The attitude of charging the bayonet as directed in the military exercise, though it has an appearance of strength and firmness, is a very weak position, from whence no other motion can well be made; being in itself as much contrary to all the rules of defence, or fencing, as for any one, after making a thrust, to remain upon the longe; the least effort made sideways on the firelock, or the body, throws the man down, or disarms him; nor can he advance, or make a push from it.'

Instead, he advocated an entirely different posture, standing more or less square on to the front and levelling the bayonet waist high: 'By our method of charging the bayonet, a man is firm against any shock, and in guard; shall see occasion, or opportunity, to defend himself, or annoy his enemy, or to advance upon him, if he should give way... We have given no word of command for pushing the bayonet, the motion being so natural, that one in action can scarce avoid doing it properly; besides no particular direction can be given about it, as every man must watch his time, and the opening which his enemy gives him, to make his push.'

Windham's method - which he rather grudgingly admitted to be similar to, if not the same as, that practised in the Prussian army - in effect wrought a minor revolution in infantry tactics and was adopted as part of the 1764 Regulations. The old-style bayonet drill, as described by Bland, was essentially a defensive one, and effective only when practised en masse. On the other hand, the new Norfolk/Prussian drill now made it possible, for the first time, to move beyond the relatively static firefight and instead conduct rapid advances - or charges - at bayonet point. This was to prove particularly important during the American War of Independence, when bayonet charges often proved more effective than prolonged firefights, particularly against an enemy who had the unsporting habit of firing from behind cover.

Simcoe's remarks upon the subject are particularly interesting: 'A light corps, augmented as the Queen's Rangers was, and employed in the duties of an outpost, had no pportunity of being instructed in the general discipline of the army, nor indeed was it necessary: the most important duties, those of vigilance, activity and patience of fatigue, were best learnt in the field; a few motions of the manual exercise were thought sufficient; they were carefully instructed in those of firing, but above all, attention was paid to inculcate the use of the bayonet, and a total reliance on that weapon.'

The officers were 'to pay great attention to the instruction of their men in charging with their bayonets, in which case, the charge was never to be less than three hundred yards, gradually increasing in celerity from its first outset, taking great care that the grand division has its ranks perfectly close, and the pace adapted to the shortest men. The soldier is, particularly, to be taught, to keep his head well up, and erect: it is graceful, on all occasions, but absolutely necessary if an enemy dare stand the charge; when the British soldier, who fixes with his eye the attention of his opponent, and, at the same instant, pushes with his bayonet without looking down on its point, is certain of conquest'.

Simcoe's insistence on using the bayonet only emphasises once again the very real distinction in the 18th century between a light infantry/partisan corps and the trained bodies of skirmishers which would prove to be of such importance during the Napoleonic Wars.

RIGHT **The pinacle of his profession: Ensign c.1745. Holding the lowest commissioned rank, this mature looking officer is clearly a promoted NCO rather than a newly joined young subaltern. [Author's collection]**

# PLATE COMMENTARY

## A: PRIVATE, 8TH (KING'S) REGIMENT, 1748

General Edward Wolfe's 8th Foot played a crucial role in the battle of Culloden just two years before the Swiss artist David Morier painted the grenadier upon which this reconstruction is based. Initially they were posted on the left of the second line, but at the crisis of the battle the 8th spearheaded General Huske's counter-attack which sealed off the Jacobite penetration of the front line. Having briskly marched on to the flank of the Jacobite assault column, they then proceeded to fire off six rounds a man at point-blank range before the rebels broke. Allowing for a hit rate of some 10 per cent at this distance, the 324 rank and file must have inflicted something in the region of 200 casualties on the rebels in the space of just two minutes, losing in return only Ensign Bruce wounded.

After the battle they remained for only a short time in Scotland before being ordered to Flanders in August 1746. In November 1748, with the war over, they were then ordered to be placed on the Irish establishment, only for the order to be revoked ten days later in favour of a posting to Gibraltar.

**The Manual Exercise 1764, demonstrated by a reconstructed officer of 1/Royals c.1794. This sequence had to be performed competently both by officers and soldiers before being 'passed by the adjutant' as properly trained. The whole battalion also had to demonstrate the same motions in its annual inspec-tion, before moving on to the 'evolutions', or maneouvres, and firings. LEFT Position of a soldier under arms – to stand straight and firm upon his legs; head turned to the right; heels close; toes a little turned out; the belly drawn in a little, but without constraint; the breast a little projected; shoulders square to the front, and kept back; the right hand hanging straight down the side, with the palm close to the thigh; the left elbow not to be turned out from the body. CENTRE 1: Poise your firelock. RIGHT 2: Cock your firelock.**
**[All author's collection]**

**1** This battalion company soldier is dressed exactly in accordance with regulations, with a full skirted coat worn over a shirt and sleeveless waistcoat. He is distinguished from members of other regiments by the combination of facing colour – in this case blue – and regimental lace **(2)**. At this time buttons were quite plain and bore neither regimental numbers nor other designations.

The blue breeches are peculiar to Royal regiments: all other infantry units wore red breeches. The white duck gaiters were normally reserved for formal guard mountings and parades. In the field, more practical brown, grey or black gaiters being worn, and a Morier painting of Cumberland at Culloden clearly shows the 13th Foot in black gaiters. As late as 1742, all belts were worn over the coat, necessitating its being closed, but as a result of the experiences of campaigning in Germany and Flanders, an important change had taken place by 1748. It had been found more comfortable – and, just as importantly, much more stylish – to wear the coat open as shown here, with the waistbelt supporting both hanger and bayonet worn under the coat. Only in cold weather, when the lapels were buttoned over for the sake of warmth, was the waistbelt worn over the coat.

By 1748 most, although by no means all, grenadiers wore wings on their shoulders **(3)**. Like the brass match cases – originally used to carry a lit slow match at night – these wings had no purpose save to mark their wearer's elite status.

**4** Grenadier's cartridge box sling with match case.

The most obvious distinguishing feature of a grenadier's uniform was the ubiquitous mitre cap **(5)**. The impression given both from Morier's paintings and from metal fronted German examples of the mitre cap is that they were quite tall and imposing, but surviving examples are almost disappointingly small and shapeless. This may simply be a reflection of the age of those caps which have survived, but soldiers, and more especially elite units such as grenadiers, did have a tendency to develop individual ways of wearing their uniforms and equipment which are often quite at odds with the dictates of the regulations and what might have been intended by those who devised them in the first place. The present battered state of the surviving caps may well reflect their having been jammed on tightly in all sorts of conditions, with little or no regard to the requirements of parade ground niceties or Swiss artists. The evidence certainly suggests that the cloth mitre cap was a much more robust, practical and popular item of uniform than the bearskin example with which it was replaced in 1768.

Two other rather more practical grenadier distinctions are recorded by Morier – a belly box **(6)** carrying the additional ammunition which a grenadier often required when detached from his parent unit (grenades were no longer carried in the cartouche or cartridge box on his right hip), and a rather more robust sword – often basket hilted – than the one carried by his comrades in the battalion companies.

**7** Private's coat, 8th Foot 1742. It was cut from a very heavy weight of wool which did not require hems, and in cold weather the very full skirts could be unhooked and the lapels buttoned over for warmth. The coat was fully lined and when shabby could be taken apart and the material turned to create a fresh, clean appearance. Given fair wear and tear, this could prolong its useful life beyond the single year normally

**LEFT 3: Present. 4: Fire. Note how the soldier's weight is transferred to his left foot, and how the firelock is supported at the swell of the stock. This provides for excellent balance and allows the soldier to take proper aim.**

allowed, permitting any new clothing to be kept for Sunday best. The white worsted tape with which the coat was decorated performed a dual function. Coloured threads were normally woven into it in order to make a unique combination of lace and the rather limited range of facing colours, which would identify the wearer's regiment. At the same time, the lace served to strengthen the unhemmed edges and buttonholes.

## B: RECRUITING FOR THE 80TH FOOT, 1780

This scene, based upon a rather convincing looking sketch by Bunbury, must have been a familiar one throughout the British Isles in the 18th century. Three would-be heroes are paraded near Holyrood House in Edinburgh for inspection by the officer in charge of the recruiting party. One, with a leather apron, appears to be a disillusioned tradesman; another looks as though he is simply enlisting in search of a square meal. Like most civilians, neither of them is yet capable of carrying himself well, but the third potential recruit is unmistakably an old soldier. In 1760 Colonel Samuel Bagshawe's instructions to the recruiting parties for his 93rd Foot solemnly warned: 'None to be taken who have been in the Service Except he be under 35 years of age, the Discharges

of such men to be sent with them to the Regt. otherwise they will be supposed to have been Drumed out, & of Course will be rejected.'

Should a recruit be rejected on these grounds, or indeed for any reason at all, when he arrived at headquarters, any monies which had already been expended on him by way of subsistence, transport, lodging and his bounty had to be borne entirely by the officer who had enlisted him in the first place. For that reason alone the recruiting service was generally unpopular. There was, therefore, every possible incentive in ordinary circumstances for officers to ensure that recruits were of a suitable standard. Unfortunately the desperate need to fill the ranks in wartime frequently saw a lowering of standards.

This was particularly true when 'letters of service' were granted for the raising of whole new regiments. The worst problems arose when a unit was raised for rank – that is, when the officers' commissions depended upon their finding a certain number of recruits within a specified period. In due course, any unsuitable men might be weeded out by inspecting officers, but by that time the desired commission had often been granted and the recruiter exchanged into some other corps, or even the half-pay list.

ABOVE 5: Half-cock your firelock.

ABOVE 6: Handle your cartridge.

Sometimes, however, a city or county might be inspired or persuaded by an enterprising officer with local connections to assist in the raising of a regiment for him; in such a case the standard of recruit might be much higher. The local authorities could generally be relied upon to supplement the official bounty and to provide alcoholic entertainments and other facilities for recruiters, helping them attract a better class of volunteer. One example of this type of unit was the 80th Royal Edinburgh Volunteers, raised during the American War of Independence. Serving in the South under Lord Cornwallis (Dundas' brigade) and surrendering at Yorktown, their title was an unofficial one, and throughout their short existence they displayed the yellow facings seen here rather than the coveted blue facings of a true Royal regiment.

## C: RECRUITS DRILLING AT CHATHAM, 1791

As a rule, once a soldier had been enlisted, he was generally delivered to regimental headquarters as quickly as possible and most if not all of his initial training then took place at company level. However, this was obviously difficult to achieve if the regiment was serving overseas. In the early part of the century, drafts of recruits for such regiments were normally held in the prison-like Savoy barracks in London – or the equally unpleasant Tilbury Fort – until transport was available. Increasing imperial commitments and a sensible – if belated – recognition that a healthy soldier was much more likely to survive the Atlantic crossing led to a change in policy.

Recruits for regiments serving in the East or West Indies, Gibraltar and North America were sent instead to one of three central depots: Stirling, Kinsale and, most important of all, Chatham Barracks. There, if they passed their medical inspection and were approved, they were kitted out and received their basic training before being shipped overseas on the next available boat.

Watched by officers of the 42nd Highlanders and 21st Fusiliers, recruits for a number of regiments are being drilled at Chatham by sergeants of the footguards. At this very early stage in their training they are still learning the rudiments of marching and facings, and consequently have not yet been issued with any accoutrements. Indeed, it is more than likely that they will reach their own battalions without having fired a single shot in training.

Standing smartly in front of one squad is a 'fugelman', an experi-enced soldier whose function is to serve as a model, smartly demonstrating the required drill movements to the assembled recruits. This useful aid to instruction is still employed today. Then, as now, the sergeant prefaced the demonstration with the otherwise contradictory order to the squad: 'Do not act upon my word of command'.

Although the footguard sergeants conducting the training quite properly wear their full regimentals, the recruits are dressed in the basic kit prescribed for them in 1791: 'Every recruit enlisted for a Regiment on foreign station, when he arrives at Chatham Barracks, and is approved of, between the 10th of March and 10th of October, if not particularly ordered by the Colonel of the Regiment to have his full clothing issued to him, is to be provided with one pair of gaiter trowsers; one red jacket with sleeves [which is to button as a waistcoat, and to be large enough to admit a waistcoat to be worn under it]; having a regimental button for the sake of distinction, and also a collar, cuffs and shoulder straps, of the colour of the facing of the Regiment to which he belongs; and one round hat.

'Every recruit remaining in the Barracks after the 10th of October, is to be furnished in addition, if destined for Gibraltar or North America, with white regimental waistcoat and breeches, which are to be considered as a part of his

clothing for that year; his trowsers, on the breeches being delivered to him, to be taken into store; but to be returned to him at the time of his embarkation, to be worn over his breeches for the sake of preserving them; but if destined for the East or West Indies, he is to be furnished with one flannel waistcoat with sleeves, one pair of flannel drawers, and a second pair of gaiter trowsers.'

## D: 43RD HIGHLANDERS ON THE MARCH, 1743

This typical scene is largely based on a quite remarkable strip cartoon, drawn by a German artist, depicting the 43rd Highlanders (later the 42nd Black Watch) on the march near Mainz. Even allowing for the artist's enthusiasm to record the diversity of this spectacle, the overwhelming impression is one of informality.

The Duke of Cumberland, among others, was to issue orders confining the regimental women to the baggage (hence the pejorative term), but the frequency with which such orders were issued suggests that on long marches it was far commoner for women to accompany their husbands intermingled in the ranks. Prohibitions of this practice may not easily have been enforced when officers' wives also accompanied the regiment. Although obviously not covered by any uniform regulations it comes as no surprise to find both officers' ladies and soldiers' wives wearing cast-off regimental jackets and plaids. While such clothing was naturally easier to obtain than most, particularly on campaign, there is some evidence that wives were just as proud of their regimental identity as their menfolk.

No contemporary illustration of marching troops seems to have been complete without one or more of these large baggage wagons, seemingly grossly overloaded both with baggage and an alarming number of passengers. In theory only the sick, or pregnant women, were allowed to travel on the wagons, but in practice this rule was once again more honoured in the breach.

## E: HEAD-DRESS

**1** Reconstruction of a surviving mitre cap worn by a grenadier of Ligonier's 49th Foot (re-numbered 48th in 1749). This style of cap should have been worn by all grenadiers and fusiliers until superseded by the bearskin cap, in 1768. In practice a number of units anticipated the adoption of the bearskin by several years; to judge from paintings and inspection reports, others seem to have clung on to the mitre for as long as possible.

Originally the mitre was simply a stocking cap with a small turn-up at front and rear – the 'little flap', but by the 1740s the whole cap was stitched together and a degree of stiffening provided for the now combined front and 'little flap', in order that the cap stood upright. It appears, however, that this attempt to smarten it up was frustrated by the grenadiers' continued insistence on jamming it on to their heads as though it was still the stocking cap that had been adopted by assault troops in the previous century as a more practical alternative to the wide-brimmed hat.

**2** The 1768 Warrant laid down that grenadier caps were now 'to be of black bear-skin. On the front, the King's crest, of silver plated metal, on a black ground, with the motto *Nec aspera terrent*. A grenade on the back part, with the number of the regiment on it. The Royal Regiments, and the Six Old

ABOVE **8: Shut your pan –1st shut your pan briskly, drawing the right arm at this motion towards your body, holding the cartridge fast in your hand; turn the piece round to the loading position with the lock to the front, and the muzzle the height of the chin, bringing the right hand behind the muzzle; both feet kept fast in this motion.**

Corps, are to have the crest and grenade, and also the other particulars as hereafter specified. The badge of the Royal Regiments is to be white, and set on or near the top of the back part of the cap. The height of the cap [without the bearskin which reaches beyond the top] to be twelve inches'.

Fusiliers were ordered to have similar caps, 'but not so high; and not to have the grenade on the back part'. To judge by portraits, most regiments readily complied with the order to place any special badges on the rear, but this was far from universally observed. A contemporary caricature by John Kay shows a grenadier of the 1st Royals with what appears to be a St. Andrew badge on the cap plate; another illustration 'drawn from the life' by Agostino Brunyas shows a grenadier of the 6th in the West Indies with that regiment's antelope badge, again displayed on the front; while yet another portrait of an officer of the 23rd Royal WELCH Fusiliers reveals a cap with no plate at all and the Prince of Wales' feathers badge worn smack in the middle of the cap.

ABOVE **9: Charge with cartridge.**

ABOVE **10: Draw your rammer.**

**3** Although they were originally ordered by the 1768 Warrant to wear a leather cap with a black bearskin front, pioneers generally wore the same grenadier cap, adorned with this striking red plate indicating their status. Drummers also had a special pattern of plate displaying drums and other martial trophies on the usual black lacquered background.

**4** Light infantry cap, 6th Foot, after sketches by Loutherberg. Made of hardened leather and further strengthened by three black iron chains around the crown, this style appears to have been the officially approved pattern when light companies were introduced, in 1771. It may have had a turned-up peak and back flap, though this is not entirely clear from Loutherberg's sketches.

**5** The all too evident unsuitability of the 'chain cap', as it was

called, soon led to a number of more of less unofficial modifications at regimental level. This particular cap, again copied from sketches by Loutherberg, was worn by the light company of the 69th Foot. A small peak has been added to what appears to be the standard 'chain cap' in order to shade the eyes, and a fairly substantial flap added to the rear, to be turned down to protect the neck in bad weather. While this style was a definite improvement on the original design it must still have been considered less than satisfactory, for a 1789 inspection report on the 69th noted that the light infantry caps were made of felt rather than leather.

**6** The process of modification is carried a stage further in this cap worn by the 5th Foot's light company. Once again there's a peak at the front to shade the eyes and a slightly smaller flap at the rear, but now the crown is surmounted by a metal

ABOVE **11: Ram down your cartridge.**

ABOVE **12: Return your rammer - return the rammer, bringing up the piece with the left hand to the shoulder, seizing it with the right hand under the cock, keeping the left hand fast at the swell, turning the body square to the front.**

comb and horsehair mane in light dragoon style. The figure of St. George and the Dragon carried on the front is the regiment's 'ancient' badge; another very similar cap belonging to the 9th Foot light company bears that regiment's Britannia badge.

**7** This wholly unauthorised leather cap appears to have been worn by the light company of Lambton's 68th Foot in the early 1770s. Superficially resembling the chain cap in some respects, it bears Lambton's own crest on the front – a practice specifically forbidden by successive clothing warrants.

## F: PRIVATE, 2/LIGHT INFANTRY, 1777

**1** This soldier belongs to one of eight provisional battalions formed by General Howe in 1776, in preparation for the invasion of Long Island. All the flank companies – that is, grenadiers and light infantry – were detached from their parent units and formed into the 1st-4th Grenadiers and 1st-4th Light Infantry. In both cases, the small 4th battalions were drawn entirely from the Highland regiments. With some minor changes in their composition as the parent regiments were moved in and out of theatre, these 'flank battalions' stayed together for the rest of the war. Initially, at least, the 2nd Light Infantry comprised companies drawn from the following units: 40th, 43rd, 44th, 45th, 49th, 52nd, 55th, 63rd and 64th Regiment of Foot. Most of these units as it happens had green facings, but others had white, buff and yellow facings, so that the lack of the usual facing coloured cuffs and other

ABOVE LEFT **13: Shoulder your firelock – the 'under arms' position.**

ABOVE CENTRE **14: Rest your firelock.**

ABOVE RIGHT **15: Order your firelock. (NB The following motions are omitted – 16: Ground your firelock; 17: Take up your firelock; 18: Rest your firelock; 19: Shoulder your firelock.)**

distinctions on the soldiers' jackets was presumably intended to create a degree of uniformity. How the various flank battalions then distinguished themselves one from another is not clear, although since the small 4th battalions of grenadiers and light infantry were both very substantially made up of the Highland flank companies, they at least were easily recognisable.

It is one of the more widespread myths surrounding the American War of Independence that the British Redcoat was greatly hampered in the struggle by having to wear a tight and uncomfortable uniform which was totally unsuited to active service anywhere, let alone in the North American wilderness. As this figure, based on paintings by Xavier Della Gatta, reveals, the reality was actually very different. The heavy wool coat has been replaced by a short, single-breasted round jacket devoid of any decoration, and the tight knee-breeches and gaiters by a light and comfortable pair of duck gaiter trousers. The impractical light infantry cap and almost equally impractical cocked hat have been replaced by a rather disreputable looking slouched hat.

Although this order of dress clearly did not entirely

supersede the clothing prescribed in the 1768 Warrant, and its use may at first have been confined to the southern campaigns, it eventually had a profound influence on the development of the British army's uniforms. The same uniform was ultimately to be worn in both the East and the West Indies and, albeit with certain comparatively minor modifications, by all British infantrymen after 1797.

**2** Another, more short-lived innovation, which made its first appearance on the Pennsylvania battlefields in 1777, was the Ferguson breechloader. Spinning the lever forming the trigger guard opened a screw plug and enabled the soldier to push a ball and the required quantity of powder directly into the breech. In bad weather four aimed rounds a minute were demonstrated to be possible; perhaps twice as many in optimum conditions. A ranger company was raised to try the

ABOVE LEFT **20: Secure your firelock. 21: Shoulder your firelock.**

ABOVE CENTRE **22: Fix your bayonet. 23: Shoulder your firelock.**

ABOVE RIGHT **24: Present your arms. 25: To the right face. 26: To the right face. 27: To the right about face.**

new weapon out in the field, but the experiment was abruptly terminated after Ferguson (at that time a captain in the 70th Foot) was wounded at the Brandywine. The rifle's subsequent demise is popularly attributed to the conservatism of British generals, but modern tests have revealed that the breech screw mechanism is susceptible to fouling, and under battlefield conditions it is likely to have become inoperable after a relatively short time.

**3** Cartridge making: a piece of 'cartridge paper', a .75 calibre ball, weighing in at 12 to the pound (hence 12 bore) and 70 grains of black powder, all tied together with thread.

**4** Combination tool.

**5** Cartridge box with regimental badge – this was the universal pattern used by those regiments who had no 'ancient

BELOW **28: To the left face. 29: To the left face. 30: To the left about face. 31: Shoulder your firelock.**

badge' such as the George and Dragon of the 5th Foot.

**6** Tin canteen.

**7** Powder horn attached to a moose-hair tumpline.

**8** Duck haversack – in theory to be used for carrying rations, but occasionally used in place of a knapsack, and typical small items of personal kit; (a) whale bone pipe; (b) shaving kit; (c) comb; (d) purse; and (e) folded blade.

**9** Cutaway of cartridge box emphasising the hidden compartment holding cleaning equipment and spare cartridge making materials.

**10** Front, back and side-views of bayonet scabbard.

## G: SKIRMISH AT ZIERENBERG, 1760

The heavy raid by Allied forces on the French post at Zierenberg in the early hours of the morning of 6 September 1760 was a textbook example of the kind of operation regularly undertaken by light troops in the 18th century. The Erbprinz of Brunswick selected ten squadrons of cavalry and six battalions of infantry for the purpose. Of those six, three were British: the 20th Foot; Maxwell's Grenadiers – a provisional battalion made up of the grenadier companies of the 12th, 20th, 23rd, 25th, 37th and 51st Foot; and 150 men of the newly raised 87th Highlanders.

Approaching the town the cavalry were ordered to throw a cordon around it and guard all the likely approaches while the three German battalions took up a covering position at Lahr, some three miles to the north. Thus the actual assault fell to the three British battalions alone, commanded by Major General John Griffin. At 2am they approached the gates. They were fired upon by a French outpost, overran it with the bayonet and pressed straight on into the town itself. There they found the French, alerted by the shooting, tumbling into the streets in their nightshirts. A hundred years earlier an anonymous chronicler of the English Civil War wrote: 'Tis the terriblest thing in the world to have an enemy fall into one's quarters by night. Nothing resembles more the last Resurrection and Judgement.' And so it proved: as the Redcoats rushed in with fixed bayonets the French suffered no fewer than 120 killed and wounded. Another 400, including the governor, were later taken prisoner.

By 4am General Griffin was on his way out again, pausing only to rescue Colonel Preston of the Scots Greys, whose rather spirited horse had jumped him into the moat. By 10am the whole force was safely back in its base at Warburg with an impressive haul of horses, prisoners and some loot. In contrast to the substantial French losses, British casualties in the affair were extremely light: four men killed and nine wounded, including General Griffin himself. 'Blue on blue' or 'friendly fire' incidents are nothing new, of course, and it seems that in the darkness and confusion Griffin had been bayoneted – though happily not very seriously – by one of his own men.

## H: 37TH FOOT AT THE BATTLE OF CULLODEN, 1746

A surprising number of eyewitness accounts of this action, written by British officers and even ordinary soldiers, have survived, allowing the minor tactics employed there to be reconstructed in unusual detail. Rather usefully, two of the accounts were written by members of Monro's 37th Foot. One, by a grenadier officer, relates how his platoon was almost overrun and makes the important comment that the men of his regiment were disinclined to take prisoners that day because it was firmly believed that a number of their officers had been murdered in cold blood by the rebels at the battle of Falkirk three months before.

A more valuable account was written by an unknown corporal: 'On the 16th [April] in the Forenoone, when we came within 300 Yards of the Rebels, they began to play their Cannon very briskly upon us; but as soon as we saw them pointed, we stoop'd down and the Balls flew over our Heads. Two Pieces of our Cannon play'd from our Left to their Right,

which kill'd many of them, and made their whole Body determine to come down upon our Left, compos'd of Barrel's, Monro's, and the Scots Fusiliers. When we saw them coming towards us in great Haste and Fury, we fired at about 50 Yards Distance, which made Hundreds fall; notwithstanding which, they were so numerous, that they still advanced, and were almost upon us before we had loaden again. We immediately gave them another full Fire and the Front Rank charged their Bayonets Breast high, and the Center and Rear Ranks kept up a continual Firing, which, in half an Hour's Time, routed their whole Army. Only Barrel's Regiment and ours was engaged, the Rebels designing to break or flank us; but our Fire was so hot, most of us having discharged nine Shot each, that they were disappointed.'

The reference to the front rank men standing fast with charged bayonets, protecting the two ranks behind while they carried on loading and firing, is extremely interesting and is supported by a letter from an officer in Wolfe's 8th Foot. He

BELOW **32: Charge your bayonet. 33: Shoulder your firelock.**

relates that his regiment also 'plied them with continual fire from our rear and fixt bayonets in front'. Similarly, David Morier's celebrated painting *Incident in the Rebellion* shows only the front rank of Barrel's 4th Foot charging their bayonets.

Although a more widely reported innovation was the instruction for each man to thrust at the Highlander approaching to his right rather than the one coming directly at him – thus bypassing his targe or defensive shield, its effectiveness is at best questionable, if only because most Jacobite soldiers were in fact armed with firelocks and bayonets. Even the swordsmen were reported to have abandoned their targes during the abortive night march which preceded the battle. The diagram on page 9 shows that the alteration in aim was very easily accomplished, but the decision to rely on the front rank bayonets while the rest continued firing was probably more decisive.

Standing next to Barrell's 4th Foot, who were overrun by the Highland assault, the 37th suffered comparatively heavy casualties at Culloden. Indeed, they had no fewer than 14 killed and 68 wounded, losses second only to the badly mauled 4th Foot. The survival rate of the wounded was depressingly low. Indeed, a Lieutenant Dally included in the official list of wounded was dead by the next morning and only 19 others afterwards claimed pensions on the strength of wounds received at Culloden. Their injuries, as recorded in the Chelsea Hospital registers, make instructive reading.

William Gill was shot through the right elbow; John Davidson was disabled in the left hand and shoulder; Thomas Grant was disabled in both thighs while Edward McMullen from Dublin was chillingly described as being disabled in several parts of his body. Luke Cunningham, a blacksmith from Limerick, was shot through the body and John Guest disabled in the right arm. Charles McLeland was shot in the right ankle, John Dollaway was disabled in the left thigh and William Ashmore disabled in the left hand and shoulder. John Tovey, 55 years of age and described as having been 'born in the army', had his jaw shot away. Arthur Buchan was disabled in the right thigh, while Thomas Lowns and Robert Farrington were both disabled in the left leg. John Perry and Richard Moulton were disabled in the right leg. Both John Hawson and Thomas Griffith were shot in the left knee, while William Irwin was simply said to have lost the use of his left leg. Most intriguingly of all, Isaac Gregg was described as having been 'disabled by a fall at Culloden'.

Nearly all of these men were fairly old as soldiers go. At 21, William Ashmore was the youngest, and 55-year-old John Tovey was the oldest. Most were from late 20s to early 40s, suggesting that as mature men they belonged to the grenadier company. This is certainly known to have been hard hit, and the unknown grenadier officer reported losing no fewer than 18 killed and wounded in his platoon alone, which must just about have wiped it out.

An analysis of wounds by type and location is of little value in this case since these obviously represent only the survivable wounds. However, what is of interest is the fact that although for the most part injured in the arm or leg, none of them were amputees. This suggests a very low survival rate for those unfortunate enough to require surgery. Indeed, it appears from the Chelsea registers that only three men out of all the wounded from Culloden survived the amputation of a limb.

## I: INFANTRY WEAPONS

**1** Long land pattern firelock with the original wooden ramrod and 46in. barrel. This was the original pattern of firelock, generally referred to as the 'Brown Bess', and was issued to most infantry regiments until officially superseded by the 42in. barrelled short land pattern in 1768. In practice, it continued to be used for some considerable time afterwards, and manufacture of this pattern only ceased as late as 1797.

**1a** Modifications for iron ramrod. The long land pattern was originally set up with a brass-tipped wooden ramrod, but from the 1720s there was a gradual changeover to iron ramrods. This necessitated the development of a quite different set of ramrod pipes, including the distinctive trumpet shaped fore-pipe and the addition of a tail-pipe.

**1b** Lock detail.

**2** Sword hilt of the so-called 1751 pattern. There was no real regulation of infantry swords since they were provided by the colonel. This style is seen in a number of Morier's grenadier paintings, hence the erroneous '1751' date. The infantry sword seems to have been much less highly regarded in the British army than in continental ones. German soldiers in particular regarded it as a status symbol, but the British soldier appears to have looked on it as an unmitigated nuisance – particularly since he had to pay for it out of stoppages from his subsistence – and it very soon disappeared.

**3** Typical basket-hilted grenadier hanger. For some reason the grenadier company tended to sport swords with basket hilts and curved or slightly curved blades.

**4** Infantry hanger and scabbard – the so-called '1742' pattern. This particular style is worn by most of the figures in the 1742 Cloathing Book – hence the description. Survival rates for this style appear to be higher than those of the '1751' pattern, suggesting that it was in much wider use.

## J: AFTER THE BATTLE, GUILFORD COURT-HOUSE, 1781

Fought on 15 March 1781, this was one of the most fiercely contested battles of the American War of Independence. General Nathaniel Greene's numerically superior American army was eventually defeated and driven from the field, but in the process General Cornwallis' small British army was so crippled as to be quite unable to pursue and destroy the Americans.

The British Redcoats had not eaten for over 24 hours before the battle, and even then it had been only a miserable four ounces of very lean beef and the same quantity of flour. Moreover, they had marched 12 miles to the battlefield on empty stomachs before fighting the gruelling two-hour engagement that same day. Not surprisingly, by the end of it they were utterly exhausted and quite unable even to recover all of their own wounded before night fell. No fewer than 93 British dead and 413 wounded lay scattered over the battlefield, together with an unknown, but probably much smaller, number of American casualties. To make matters worse, the sky began to cloud over towards the end of the battle and shortly after the Americans withdrew from the field, the heavens opened.

In order to catch Greene in the first place, Cornwallis had destroyed his baggage train and with it the army's tents. Consequently, neither the survivors of the battle nor the wounded found any shelter that night, and the resultant horror was afterwards described by a wounded Guards officer, Major General Charles O'Hara: 'I never did and I hope I never shall experience two such days and nights as those immediately after the battle. We remained on the very ground on which it had been fought, covered with dead, with dying and with hundreds of wounded, rebels as well as our own. A violent and constant rain that lasted above forty hours made it equally impracticable to remove or administer the smallest comfort to our wounded.'

## K: 21ST FOOT ENCAMPED, ROERMOND, HOLLAND, 1748

As the War of the Austrian Succession ground to an exhausted halt in the spring of 1748, the Swiss artist David Morier visited the British army in its camp at Roermond in Holland. His purpose was to carry on with the commission from the Duke of Cumberland to paint a cavalry trooper and a grenadier from every regiment in the army. Evidently, the first canvasses had already been painted in the artist's London studio that winter, but now he took advantage of the good weather and absence of hostilities to execute a large canvas depicting the Royal Artillery as well as a further five grenadier paintings (see MAA 285, King George's Army 1740-93, Vol.1). Although the chief interest in these paintings has traditionally lain in the uniform details they record, the backgrounds to this particular group are equally important in providing a series of unposed vignettes of off-duty soldiers, wives and children going about their affairs in the tent lines.

On the outbreak of war with France in February 1793, wedge tents were issued 14 to a company – roughly five men to a tent. This seems to have been pretty constant throughout this period. In May 1759, the 42nd Highlanders were ordered to be 'made up into Messes allowing 6 men to a tent and the Camp necessaries to be given out accordingly'. In 1793 at least a tin kettle and hatchet were issued with each tent, together with two blankets – presumably to replace or be spread on top of the thick carpet of grass, leaves or straw normally laid on tent floors.

Sergeants were 'to lay always in the front tents of their different companies'. Officers, on the other hand, had to purchase their own tents – one was allowed for each captain, although according to the orderly book of the 42nd Highlanders in 1759, subalterns were expected to share one tent between two: 'The officers to provide themselves furthwith in tents according to the pattern tent which is to be seen at the tent makers, and to have those tents ready to be shown to the Commanding Officer on the tenth of March. No more than one tent will be allowed for two subalterns, they are therefore to divide themselves and bespeak their tents accordingly as none is to be bespoke for them.'

The 21st Foot was another Culloden regiment, losing just seven wounded there, and as fusiliers all ranks were of course supposed to wear mitre caps. The design on the grenadier cap is taken from Morier, while the slightly different style displayed by the battalion company man standing on the left is taken from the 1742 Cloathing Book. Others wear what appears to have been a very common style of forage cap of the period.

ABOVE **34: Advance your arms. 35: Shoulder your firelock.**

## L: PRIVATE, 1/ROYALS, 1789

On 13 June 1789 1/Royals (later 1st Battalion, Royal Scots) were reviewed by Major General Robert Prescott at Charles Fort, Kinsale. The men were reported to be 'of a good size, young and stout, clean under arms, well dressed, steady and attentive'. His comments on the comparative youth of the soldiers were supported by a table which shows that 48 men were aged between 18 and 19; 148 between 20 and 24; 116 between 25 and 29; 63 between 30 and 34; and only 29 between 35 and 39. Since the figures for the upper age groups obviously included the sergeants and the grenadiers, who were generally the more mature men in the battalion, the average age of the rank and file in the battalion companies must have been correspondingly lower. As for their country of origin, 240 men (unsurprisingly) were Scots; of the remainder, 84 were English and 89 Irish. These figures broadly reflected the grenadier company at the time of muster, at Limerick in

comparatively new. Hats were well cocked and 'according to the King's regulations', while black spatterdashes were worn according to orders. Prescott considered the clothing to be 'good, well fitted, perfectly agreeable to King's Regulations'.

All in all, it was a very favourable report, and it found the battalion fit for service. So on 29 January 1790 they embarked for Jamaica, and ultimately to their effective destruction, on San Domingo.

**(1)** Based on a watercolour sketch by Dayes, this soldier is dressed for home service according to the King's Regulations. Apart from minor regimental idiosyncrasies such as the sideburns – a feature which crops up in other contemporary illustrations of regimental personnel – he provides an excellent picture of the ordinary British soldier on the eve of the great war with France. Although a grenadier, as shown by his laced shoulder wings, he wears an ordinary cocked hat in place of the unpopular bearskin cap prescribed in 1768. Judging by other contemporary illustrations and inspection reports, this was very common practice.

He is armed with a Short Land Pattern firelock and bayonet. Both the sword and the brass match-case had been abolished after the American War of Independence on the grounds that they were useless encumbrances and were never carried by grenadiers in action – the battalion companies had officially lost their swords in 1768, but had ceased wearing them many years before.

Notwithstanding these sensible measures, the uniform was generally rather too tight and uncomfortable, and although the 2nd Battalion of the Royals appears to have worn it when they went to Toulon in 1794, the 1st Battalion, which was fighting at the same time against republican rebels on San Domingo, would have resembled the far more sensibly dressed soldier of Plate F.

**(2)** Regimental breastplates: (a) officer 1/Royals; (b) private 1/Royals, and button loop of regimental lace. The button itself bore the device:   FO1OT

**(3)** Breeches: normally made from white wool, they could be replaced in warmer weather by lighter garments made of duck or linen. Note the fall front which superseded the earlier fly front under the 1768 Warrant.

**(4)** Shirt, with typical cuff-link contrived from two buttons.

**(5)** Half gaiters as worn by light infantry and by other soldiers in warm weather or upon long marches.

**(6)** Buckled shoes.

**(7)** Bayonet scabbard and belt.

# BIBLIOGRAPHY

*Advice to the Officers of the British Army, with the Addition of some hints to the Drummer and Private Soldier (1782),* (2nd Edn. London 1948)

Atkinson, C.J., Jenkins Ear, *The Austrian Succession War and the Fortyfive.* (Journal of the Society for Army Historical Research, vol.22)

Aytoun, *James Redcoats in the Caribbean* (Blackburn 1984)

Bailey, D.W., *British Military Longarms 1714-1865* (London 1986)

Blackmore, H.L., *British Military Firearms 1650-1850* (2nd Edn. London 1994)

Bland, Humphrey, *Treatise of Military Discipline,* (1727)

Boatner, Mark, *Encyclopedia of the American Revolution* (Mechanicsburg PA 1994)

Bowler, R. Arthur, *Logistics and the Failure of the British Army in America,* (Princeton NJ 1975)

Bruce, A, *The Purchase System in the British Army,* (Royal Historical Society 1980)

Bulloch, J.M., *Territorial Soldiering in North-East Scotland* (New Spalding Club, Aberdeen 1914)

Chandler, David, *The Art of Warfare in the Age of Marlborough* (London 1976)

Darling, A.D., *Redcoat and Brown Bess,* (Ottawa 1970)

Fuller, J.F.C., *British Light Infantry in the Eighteenth Century* (London 1925)

*General Wolfe's Instructions to Young Officers* (London 1768)

*Gentleman Volunteer's Pocket Companion describing the various motions of the Footguards in the Manual Exercise,* (London 1745)

Grant, George, *The New Highland Discipline,* (London 1757)

Guy, A.J., *Oeconomy and Discipline: Officership and Administration in the British Army 1714-63* (Manchester 1985)

Guy, A.J., *Colonel Samuel Bagshawe and the Army of George II, 1731-1762,* (Army Records Society 1990)

Houlding, J.A., *Fit for Service: The Training of the British Army 1715-1795,* (Oxford 1981)

Hughes, B.P., *Firepower: Weapons Effectiveness on the Battlefield 1630-1850,* (London 1974)

Katcher, Philip, *Armies of the American Wars 1753-1815* (London 1975)

Lens, Bernard, *The Granadiers Exercise 1735* (London 1967)

*The Manual Exercise as Ordered by His Majesty in 1764, together with Plans and Explanations of the Method generally Practis'd at Reviews and Field Days &c.*

Peterkin, Ernest, *The Exercise of Arms in the Continental Infantry,* (Bloomfield Ontario 1989)

Prebble, John, *Mutiny* (London 1975)

Reid, Stuart, *Like Hungry Wolves: Culloden Moor 16th April 1746,* (London 1994)

Reid, Stuart, *1745: A Military History,* (Staplehurst 1996)

Savory, Sir Reginald, *His Brittanic Majesty's Army in Germany during the Seven Years War,* (Oxford 1966)

Simcoe, Lt.Col. J.G., *A History of the Operations of a Partisan Corps called THE QUEEN'S RANGERS* (New York 1844)

Stewart, David, *Sketches of the Highlanders of Scotland* (Edinburgh 1822)

Strachan, Hew, *British Military Uniforms 1768-1796* (London 1975)

Windham, William, *A Plan of Discipline Composed for the Use of the Militia of the County of Norfolk,* (London 1759)

# GLOSSARY

ADDITIONAL COMPANY: regimental depot unit

ADJUTANT: battalion staff officer responsible for drill, discipline and administration

AMERICAN TROUSERS: combination breeches and gaiters

BATTALION: tactical unit comprising upwards of four companies.

BATTALION COMPANIES: non-specialist centre companies in a battalion

BLACKBALL: wax composition used for blackening shoes and other leatherwork

BLUE BONNEt: flat, knitted bonnet worn by Highland units, invariably blue.

BOUNTY: payment made or credited to soldier on enlistment

BREASTPLATE: oval or rectangular plate serving as a belt buckle on the bayonet belt and normally bearing a regiment's badge, title and/or number.

CARBINE: firearm with .69 bore - term relates to bore not to barrel length

COMPANY: administrative unit comprising three officers and between thirty and one hundred soldiers

DRAFTING: transfer of soldiers from one battalion to another

FIRELOCK: generic term for infantry firearms, invariably used instead of a musket.

FLANK COMPANY: Grenadier and/or Light Infantry company, so termed because posted on flanks of a battalion when formally drawn up.

FLANK BATTALION: provisional unit made up of Grenadier or Light Infantry companies detached from their parent units.

FUSIL: lightweight firelock carried by officers and sergeants

GAITER TROUSERS: see American Trousers

HANGER: short, generally curved sword

HATMAN: soldier belonging to one of the centre or battalion companies, so named because wearing a hat instead of a cap as worn by the flank companies

HAVERSACK: coarse linen bag for carrying rations

HUMMEL BONNET: any bonnet lacking feathers or other adornment

INDEPENDENT COMPANY: unregimented company, used either for recruiting or garrison duties

INVALID: soldier classed as unfit for service in a marching regiment, but still capable of serving in a garrison unit

KILMARNOCK BONNET: knitted bonnet blocked upwards into drum shape, always blue, but usually with checquered band around sides.

KNAPSACK: bag carried on back, containing soldier's personal kit

MANUAL EXERCISE: basic weapon handling drill

MATCH-CASE: brass tube theoretically used by grenadiers for carrying the slow- match needed to light the grenade fuse - in practice obsolete and decorative

NECESSARIES: consumables and small items of equipment required to be bought by soldiers, either privately or through deductions from their subsistence.

OFF RECKONINGS: that part of a soldier's pay made over to his Colonel for the purchase of clothing

PLATOON (1): tactical sub-unit for fire-control purposes, generally between twenty and thirty strong.

PLATOON (2): slang term for volley

PLATOONING: slang term for firing by platoons

REGIMENT: soldier's administrative and spiritual home. In British service almost invariably comprising a single battalion. In the few cases where second battalions existed, they were to all intents and purposes seperate units, not tactical sub-divisions as in continental armies

REGIMENTAL: slang – conforming to regimental standing orders

ROLLER: rolled-up neck-cloth

SQUIB: blank round

STOCK: cloth band fastened around neck with a buckle, in place of roller

SUBSISTENCE: that part of soldier's pay allowed to him for the purchase of food, necessaries and anything else which he could afford.

VESTRY MEN: short service conscripts rounded up by parish officials

VOLUNTEER: aspiring officer, serving in the ranks in hopes of being appointed to a free commission

WATCHCOAt: heavy greatcoat, ankle-length and often with a hood, usually issued only to sentries.

## Notes sur les planches en couleur

**A** Simple soldat, 8e Régiment (Régiment du Roi), 1748.**1** Ce soldat d'un bataillon de compagnie porte un uniforme totalement conforme au règlement : un manteau à grandes basques sur une chemise et un gilet sans manches. Il se différencie des membres des autres régiments par la couleur de ses revers (bleu dans ce cas précis) et par les galons de son régiment. A cette époque, les boutons étaient assez simples et ne portaient ni le numéro du régiment ni d'autres désignations. La culotte bleue est spécifique aux régiments royaux : toutes les autres unités d'infanterie portaient une culotte rouge. Les guêtres blanches étaient normalement réservées aux gardes et parades officielles. Le manteau est ouvert comme illustré ici et la ceinture soutient le coutelas et la baïonnette portée sous le manteau. **(2)** Distinctions des grenadiers. **(3)** Manteaux de simples soldats en 1742. Le Livre des Uniformes et la Liste des Armées de Millan révèlent que le 8e avaient originellement des parements jaunes. On ne connaît pas la date à laquelle on passa aux parements bleus et au nouveau type de galon illustrés par Morier en 1748.

**B** Recrutement pour le 80e Régiment d'infanterie, 1780. Cette scène, basée sur un croquis assez convaincant de Bunbury, devait être très courante au XVIIIe siècle dans toutes les îles britanniques. On fait défiler trois héros en puissance près de Holyrood House à Edimbourg avant qu'ils soient inspectés par l'officier responsable du groupe de recrutement. Le premier porte un tablier de cuir et semble être un commerçant déçu, le second semble vouloir entrer dans l'armée pour pouvoir manger à sa faim. Comme la plupart des civils, ni l'un ni l'autre n'est encore capable d'adopter une belle posture alors que la troisième recrue en puissance est sans aucun doute un ancien soldat. En 1760, les instructions du Colonel Samuel Bagshawe aux groupes de recrutement pour son 93e Régiment d'Infanterie donnaient l'avertissement suivant : "N'accepter aucune recrue de plus de 35 ans ayant déjà servi dans l'armée. Ils doivent amener leur Décharge avec eux au Régiment sans quoi on supposera qu'ils ont été expulsés et bien entendu ils seront rejetés".

**C** Recrues à l'entraînement à Chatham, 1791. En règle générale, une fois qu'un soldat s'était engagé, on l'emmenait généralement au quartier général du régiment aussi vite que possible et la plupart, sinon la totalité, de sa formation initiale se déroulait alors au niveau de la compagnie. Mais cela était évidemment difficile à faire si le régiment était en service à l'étranger. Au début du siècle, les conscriptions de recrues pour ces régiments se déroulaient normalement à la caserne Savoy à Londres, qui ressemblait à une prison, ou à Tilbury Fort (tout aussi désagréable) jusqu'à ce que les transports soient disponibles. La taille grandissante de l'empire et l'idée raisonnable (bien que tardive) comme quoi un soldat en bonne santé avait beaucoup plus de chances de survivre à la traversée de l'Atlantique provoquèrent un changement de tactique. Durant les phases initiales de leur entraînement, on leur apprend encore les rudiments de la marche et des mouvements de front et on ne leur a donc pas encore distribué leur fourniment. Il est très probable qu'ils arriveront dans leur bataillon sans avoir tiré un seul coup de feu durant leur formation.

**D** 43e Régiment de Highlanders en marche, 1743. Cette scène typique est largement inspirée d'une remarquable série de planches dessinées par un artiste allemand et qui décrit le 43e régiment de Highlanders (transformé ensuite en 42e Régiment Black Watch) en marche près de Mainz. Même si l'on prend en compte l'enthousiasme de l'artiste qui voulait enregistrer la diversité de ce spectacle, l'impression générale est celle d'un grand manque de formalité. Il semble que toutes les illustrations contemporaines de troupes en marche comportent un ou plusieurs grands chars à bagages qui semblent très surchargés de bagages et remplis d'un nombre inquiétant de passagers. En théorie, seuls les malades ou les femmes enceintes avaient le droit de voyager dans ces chars mais en pratique cette règle n'était pas souvent respectée.

**E** Couvre-chefs. **1** Reconstitution d'un calot mitré porté par un grenadier du 49e Régiment d'infanterie de Ligonier (renuméroté 48e en 1749). Ce style de couvre-chef aurait bien pu être porté par tous les grenadiers et fusiliers jusqu'à ce qu'il soit remplacé par le bonnet à poil en 1768. **2** La Loi de 1768 déclarait que les couvre-chefs des grenadiers devaient désormais "être en peau d'ours noire. A l'avant, il devait y avoir les armes du Roi, en métal argenté sur fond noir avec la devise Nec aspera terrent. Une grenade à l'arrière, sur laquelle était inscrite le numéro du régiment. Les Régiments Royaux et les Six anciens corps doivent avoir les armes et la grenade ainsi que les autres détails spécifiés. Le badge des Régiments Royaux doit être blanc et doit se trouver près du sommet de l'arrière du bonnet. La hauteur du bonnet [sans la fourrure d'ours qui dépasse en hauteur] doit être de douze pouces". **3** Bien que la Loi de 1768 ait décidé que les pionniers devaient porter un calot de cuir avec un panneau avant en peau d'ours noire, ils portaient souvent le même calot de grenadier orné de cette plaque rouge très frappante qui indiquait leur statut. **4** Calot d'infanterie légère, 6e Régiment d'Infanterie, d'après des croquis de Loutheberg. Ce couvre-chef, en cuir durci et renforcé par trois chaînes de fer noir autour de la calotte, semble avoir été le modèle officiel lorsque les compagnies légères furent introduites en 1771. **5** L'inadaptation très évidente du "calot à chaînes" comme on l'appelait, entraîna rapidement un certain nombre de modifications plus ou moins officieuses au niveau des régiments. Ce calot particulier, copié encore une fois de croquis de Loutheberg, était porté par la compagnie légère du 69e Régiment d'Infanterie. **6** Le processus de modification est poussé encore plus loin dans ce calot porté par la compagnie légère du 5e Régiment d'Infanterie. Là aussi, on remarque la visière à l'avant pour protéger les yeux du soleil et un rabat un peu plus petit à l'arrière, mais cette fois la calotte est surmontée par un peigne métallique et par une crinière de crin dans le style des dragons légers. **7** Ce calot n'a rien à voir avec les prescriptions officielles mais semble avoir été adopté par la compagnie légère du 68ème Régiment d'infanterie de Lambton vers 1770.

**F** Simple soldat, Infanterie Légère, 1777.**1** Ce soldat appartient à l'un des huit bataillons provisoires formés par le Général Howe en 1776 pour préparer l'invasion de Long Island. La plupart de ces unités avaient des parements verts mais d'autres avaient des parements blancs, grèges et jaunes. L'absence des revers habituellement de la même couleur que les parements et autres distinctions sur les vestes des soldats avait sans doute pour but de créer un certain degré d'uniformité. Le lourd manteau de laine avait été remplacé par une veste courte, ronde et à boutonnage simple sans aucune décoration et la culotte serrée et les guêtres par un pantalon léger et confortable. Le calot de l'infanterie légère, peu pratique, ainsi que le tricorne tout aussi peu pratique ont été remplacés par un chapeau mou qui n'a pas belle allure. **2** fusil Ferguson chargé par la culasse. **3** Fabrication des cartouches : un morceau de "papier à cartouches", une balle de calibre .75, 12 par livre (donc calibre 12) et 70 grains de poudre noire, liés avec du fil. **4** Outil polyvalent. **5** Badge de cartouchière. **6** Gamelle. **7** Havresac en coutil.

**G** Escarmouche à Zierenberg, 1760. Le raid des forces alliées sur le poste français de Zierenberg au petit matin le 6 septembre 1760 est un exemple-type du genre d'opérations régulièrement entreprises par les troupes légères au XVIIIe siècle. A l'approche de la ville, on commanda à la cavalerie d'installer un cordon autour de la ville et de garder les trois approches probables pendant que les trois bataillons allemands prenaient une position de couverture à Lahr, à 5km au nord environ. L'assaut direct tomba donc sur les trois bataillons britanniques seuls, commandés par le Major-Général John Griffin. Vers 10h, toutes les forces étaient de retour à leur base à Warburg avec un impressionnant coup de filet : chevaux, prisonniers et butin, alors que les Français subirent de lourdes pertes.

**H** Bataille - Le 37e Régiment d'Infanterie à Culloden, 1746. La référence aux hommes du premier rang debout avec leurs baïonnettes chargées et protégeant les deux rangs derrière eux alors qu'ils continuaient à charger et à tirer est extrêmement intéressante. Cette référence est confirmée par une lettre envoyée par un officier du 8ème Régiment d'Infanterie de Wolfe. Il raconte que son

## Farbtafeln

**A** Gefreiter, 8th (King's) Regiment, 1748. **1** Dieser Kompaniesoldat eines Bataillons ist genau vorschriftsmäßig gekleidet. Er trägt einen Waffenrock mit weitem Schoß über einem Hemd und einer ärmellosen Weste. Er unterscheidet sich von den Angehörigen anderer Regimenter durch die Kombination der Besatzfarbe - in diesem Fall blau - und der Regimentslitze. Zu dieser Zeit waren die Uniformknöpfe recht einfach und wiesen weder Regimentsnummern noch anderweitige Kennzeichen auf. Die blauen Breeches waren den königlichen Regimentern vorbehalten: Alle anderen Infanterieeinheiten trugen rote Breeches. Die weißen Segeltuchgamaschen wurden normalerweise nur bei offiziellen Gardeaufmärschen und Paraden getragen. Der Uniformrock ist wie hier gezeigt offen, und der Leibriemen dient als Befestigung für das Gehenk und das Bajonett, das unter der Jacke getragen wurde. **(2)** Unterscheidungsmerkmale eines Grenadiers. **(3)** Röcke von Gefreiten 1742. Sowohl in der Kleidervorschrift ("Cloathing Book") als auch in der Millan's Army List ist belegt, daß das 8th Regiment ursprünglich gelbe Besätze hatte. Es ist nicht bekannt, wann der Wechsel zu blauen Besätzen und einer anderen Litzenanordnung, wie sie von Morier 1748 dargestellt wurde, stattfand.

**B** Rekrutierung für das 80th Foot, 1780. Die abgebildete Szene, die auf einer recht überzeugenden Skizze von Bunbury beruht, muß im 18. Jahrhundert überall auf den Britischen Inseln ein recht vertrauter Anblick gewesen sein. In der Nähe des Holyrood House in Edinburgh läßt man drei angehende Helden aufmarschieren, damit der für die Rekrutierung zuständige Offizier sie in Augenschein nehmen kann. Bei einem der Willigen - er trägt eine Lederschürze - scheint es sich um einen desillusionierten Handwerker zu handeln; ein zweiter macht den Eindruck, als ob er sich vom Einzug ins Militär eine ordentliche Mahlzeit erhoffe. Wie die meisten Zivilisten zeigen beide noch nicht die richtige Haltung, doch der dritte potentielle Rekrut ist eindeutig ein alter Soldat. 1760 hatte Colonel Samuel Bagshawe in seinen Anordnungen für die Rekrutierausschüsse für seine 93rd Foot ausdrücklich gewarnt: "Es dürfen keine Männer rekrutiert werden, die bereits im Dienst waren, es sei denn der Betreffende ist jünger als 35 Jahre. Das Entlassungszeugnis eines solchen Bewerbers muß an das Regiment geschickt werden, ansonsten muß angenommen werden, daß der Betreffende schimpflich ausgestoßen wurde und daher abgelehnt werden muß."

**C** Drill von Rekruten in Chatham, 1791. War ein Soldat erst einmal eingezogen, wo wurde er im allgemeinen zunächst so schnell wie möglich ins Hauptquartier des Regiments überstellt. Der Großteil seiner Grundausbildung - oder auch die gesamte - fand dann auf Kompanieebene statt. Allerdings war dies offenbar schwierig, wenn das Regiment in Übersee diente. Anfang des 18. Jahrhunderts wurden Soldaten, die für diese Regimenter eingezogen worden waren, normalerweise in der Londoner Savoy-Kaserne, die eher einem Gefängnis glich, untergebracht, oder auch im ähnlich unangenehmen Tilbury Fort, bis sich eine Transportmöglichkeit ergab. Aufgrund zunehmender Verpflichtungen des Britischen Reiches und der vernünftigen - wenn auch späten - Erkenntnis, daß ein gesunder Soldat viel größere Chancen hatte, die Überquerung des Atlantiks zu überleben, kam es zu einer Änderung dieser Verfahrensweise. In diesem sehr frühen Stadium ihrer Ausbildung lernen die Rekruten noch die Grundzüge des Marschierens und der Kehrtwendung. Folglich hat man ihnen noch keinerlei militärische Ausrüstung ausgegeben. Es war in der Tat nur allzu wahrscheinlich, daß sie zu ihrem jeweiligen Bataillon stießen, ohne bei der Ausbildung je auch nur einen Schuß abgefeuert zu haben.

**D** 43rd Highlanders auf dem Marsch, 1743. Diese typische Szene beruht größtenteils auf einer recht bemerkenswerten Karikaturskizze, die von einem deutschen Zeichner angefertigt wurde. Sie zeigt die 43rd Highlanders (die spätere 42nd Black Watch) auf dem Marsch in der Nähe von Mainz. Selbst wenn man das Bestreben des Zeichners, die Vielseitigkeit dieses Spektakels einzufangen, berücksichtigt, erhält man doch einen überwältigenden Eindruck der Ungezwungenheit. Keine zeitgenössische Darstellung marschierender Truppen scheint ohne einen oder mehrere dieser großen Gepäckwagen auszukommen, die offenbar mit Gepäck und einer beängstigenden Anzahl von Passagieren ungeheuer überladen sind. Laut Vorschrift durften eigentlich nur Kranke oder schwangere Frauen auf diesen Wagen mitfahren. In der Praxis war die Einhaltung dieser Bestimmung allerdings eher die Ausnahme als die Regel.

**E** Kopfbedeckungen. **1** Nachbildung einer erhaltenen "Mitramütze", die von einem Grenadier der 49th Foot (1749 zu 48th umnumeriert) von Ligonier getragen wurde. Diese Art Mütze hätten eigentlich alle Grenadiere und Füsiliere tragen sollen, bis sie 1768 durch die Bärenfellmütze ersetzt wurde. **2** In den Vorschriften von 1768 wurde festgelegt, daß die Mützen der Grenadiere von nun an "aus schwarzem Bärenfell sein müssen. Auf der Vorderseite das Emblem des Königs aus versilbertem Metall auf schwarzem Hintergrund, mit dem Motto 'Nec aspera terrent'. Auf dem rückwärtigen Teil eine Granate mit der Nummer des Regiments darauf. Die Royal Regiments und die Six Old Corps sollen das Emblem und die Granate haben sowie die nachstehend aufgeführten besonderen Merkmale. Das Abzeichen der Royal Regiments hat weiß zu sein und ist auf beziehungsweise in der Nähe der Oberseite des rückwärtigen Teils der Mütze anzubringen. Die Höhe der Mütze [ohne das Bärenfell, das sich über den oberen Rand erhebt] soll zwölf Zoll betragen." **3** Obgleich die Vorschriften von 1768 ursprünglich das Tragen einer Ledermütze mit einem Vorderteil aus schwarzem Bärenfell vorsahen, trugen die Pioniere im allgemeinen die gleiche Grenadiermütze, die mit dieser bestechenden roten Platte als Statussymbol verziert war. **4** Mütze der leichten Infanterie, 6th Foot, nach Skizzen von Loutherberg. Die Mütze ist aus gehärtetem Leder und wurde mittels drei Ketten aus schwarzem Eisen um die Krone zusätzlich verstärkt. Diese Ausführung scheint das offiziell genehmigte Modell gewesen zu sein, als 1771 leichte Kompanien eingeführt wurden. **5** Die nur allzu ersichtliche mangelnde Eignung der sogenannten "Kettenmütze" führte schon bald zu einer Reihe mehr oder weniger offizieller Modifikationen auf Regimentsebene. Die abgebildete Mütze, ebenfalls von Loutherberg-Skizzen kopiert, wurde von der leichten Kompanie der 69th Foot getragen. **6** Bei dieser Mütze, die von der leichten Kompanie der 5th Foot getragen wurde, gingen die Abwandlungen noch einen Schritt weiter. Auch hier sieht man wieder zum Schutz der Augen einen Schirm am Vorderteil und eine etwas kleinere Klappe am rückwärtigen Teil, doch befindet sich hier auf der Krone ein Metallkamm und ein Roßhaarbusch im Stil der leichten Dragoner. **7** Diese gänzlich gegen die Vorschrift verstoßende Ledermütze wurde anscheinend in den frühen 70er Jahren des 18. Jahrhunderts von der leichten Kompanie der 68th Foot von Lambton getragen.

**F** Gefreiter, 2/leichte Infanterie, 1777. **1** Dieser Soldat gehört zu einem der acht provisorischen Bataillone, die General Howe 1776 für die Invasion von Long Island aufstellte. Ein Großteil dieser Einheiten hatten zufällig grüne Besätze, andere allerdings weiße, gelbbraune und gelbe Besätze, so daß das Fehlen der üblichen Manschetten in der Besatzfarbe und anderer Kennzeichen auf den Jacken der Soldaten wahrscheinlich darauf angelegt war, ein gewissen Maß an Einheitlichkeit zu schaffen. Der Waffenrock aus schwerem Wollstoff wurde durch eine kurze, einreihige, abgerundete Jacke ohne Verzierung ersetzt, die engen Kniehosen und Gamaschen durch leichte, bequeme Gamaschenhosen aus Segeltuch. Die unpraktische Mütze der leichten Infanterie und der fast ebenso unpraktische Dreispitz wurden durch einen eher schäbig aussehenden Schlapphut ersetzt. **2** Ferguson-Hinterlader. **3** Patronenfertigung: Ein Stück "Patronenpapier", eine 0.75 Kaliber-Kugel, von denen zwölf jeweils ein Pfund wiegen (daher auch 12 Kaliber) und 70 Körnchen schwarzes Pulver, alles mit Faden zusammengebunden. **4** Mehrzweckwerkzeug. **5** Abzeichen auf der Patronentasche. **6** Eßgeschirr aus Blech. **7** Rucksack aus Segeltuch.

**G** Scharmützel bei Zierenberg, 1760. Der schwere Überfall seitens der alliierten Streitmächte auf das französische Fort bei Zierenberg in den frühen Morgenstunden des 6. September 1760 war ein exemplarisches Beispiel für die Art von Angriff, wie ihn leichte Truppen im 18. Jahrhundert regelmäßig führten. Bei Annäherung an die Stadt wurde der Kavallerie befohlen, eine Postenkette

régiment "les soumit à un feu continu de notre arrière et de baïonnettes fixes à l'avant". Le diagramme joint montre que la modification de cible fut très facile à réaliser mais que c'est la décision de s'appuyer sur les baïonnettes du premier rang pendant que les autres continuaient à tirer qui fut sans doute plus décisive.

I Armes d'infanterie. 1 Fusil à pierre modèle Long Land avec la baguette en bois d'origine et baril de 46 pouces. 1a Modifications pour une baguette en fer. Le modèle Long Land était tout d'abord chargé avec une baguette en bois à bout de cuivre mais à partir de 1720 on passa progressivement aux baguettes de fer. 1b Détail de la gâchette. 2 Crosse d'épée du modèle 1751. 3 Coutelas de grenadier typique à poignée en panier. 4 Coutelas d'infanterie et fourreau.

J Après la bataille, Guilford Courthouse, 1781. Cette bataille, qui se disputa le 15 mars 1781, fut l'une des plus âpres de la guerre américaine d'indépendance. L'armée américaine du Général Nathaniel Greene, supérieure en effectifs, finit par être vaincue et repoussée hors du champ de bataille mais la petite armée britannique du Général Cornwallis fut tellement mutilée durant le combat qu'elle fut tout-à-fait incapable de poursuivre et détruire les Américains.

K 21ème Régiment d'Infanterie en camp, Roermond, Hollande, 1748. Lorsque la guerre de la succession autrichienne s'arrêta d'épuisement au printemps 1748, l'artiste suisse David Morier rendit visite à l'armée britannique à son camp de Roermond en Hollande. Il voulait continuer d'exécuter la commande du Duc de Cumberland, qui était de peindre un soldat de cavalerie et un grenadier de chaque régiment de l'armée.

L Simple Soldat, 1/Royals, 1789. 1 Bien qu'il s'agisse d'un grenadier, comme l'indiquent ses épaulettes lacées, il porte un tricorne ordinaire au lieu du bonnet à poil très peu aimé prescrit en 1768. Il est armé d'un fusil à pierre modèle Short Land et d'une baïonnette. 2 Plastrons de régiment : (a) officier 1/Royals ; (b) simple soldat 1/Royals et boucle à bouton en galon de régiment. Le bouton lui-même portait la devise : FO1OT 3 Culotte : normalement en laine blanche mais elle pouvait être remplacée par temps plus chaud par un vêtement plus léger en coutil ou en lin. Notez le panneau avant déboutonnable qui remplace la braguette, selon les prescriptions de 1768. 4 Chemise, avec bouton de manchette typique fabriqué à partir de deux boutons. 5 Demi-guêtres portées par l'infanterie légère et par d'autres soldats par temps chaud ou durant les longues marches. 6 Chaussures à boucle. 7 Fourreau et ceinture de baïonnette.

um die Ortschaft zu bilden und alle möglichen Anlaufpunkte zu bewachen. Unterdessen bezogen die drei deutschen Bataillone eine Deckungsstellung bei Lahr, etwa 5km nördlich. Somit blieb der eigentliche Angriff allein den drei britischen Bataillonen unter dem Kommando von Major General John Griffin überlassen. Um 10 Uhr morgens war das gesamte Heer bereits wieder sicher zurück in seinem Stützpunkt in Warburg, und zwar mit einer eindrucksvollen Beute an Pferden, Gefangenen und einigem Plündergut. Die Franzosen hingegen hatten schwere Verluste erlitten.

H Schlacht - 37th Foot bei Culloden, 1746. Der Verweis auf die Soldaten des vorderen Rangs, die mit gezogenem Bajonett dem Ansturm standhalten und die beiden dahinterstehenden Ränge während des Ladens und Feuerns schützen, ist äußerst interessant und wird auch von einem Brief eines Offiziers in Wolfes 8th Foot belegt. Er schreibt, sein Regiment habe "sie auch mit anhaltendem Feuer aus unseren hinteren Rängen überschüttet und mit den festen Bajonetten im vorderen Rang bekämpft". Das ergänzende Diagramm zeigt, daß die Änderung der Zielrichtung leicht zu vollziehen war, daß aber wahrscheinlich die Entscheidung, sich auf die Bajonette des vorderen Rangs zu verlassen, während die übrigen Soldaten weiterfeuerten, ausschlaggebend war.

I Infanteriewaffen. 1 Muskete des langen Landmodells mit dem ursprünglichen hölzernen Ladestock und 46 Zoll-Lauf. 1a Modifikationen für den Ladestock aus Eisen. Das lange Landmodell wurde ursprünglich mit einem hölzernen Ladestock mit Messingspitze geladen, allerdings ging man ab etwa 1720 allmählich zu Ladestöcken aus Eisen über. 1b Schloß im Detail. 2 Schwertheft des sogenannten 1751er Modells. 3 Typisches Grenadier-Gehenk mit Korbheft. 4 Infanterie-Gehenk und Degenscheide.

J Nach der Schlacht, Gerichtsgebäude in Guilford, 1781. Die Schlacht vom 15. März 1781 war einer der heftigsten Kämpfe im amerikanischen Unabhängigkeitskrieg. General Nathaniel Greenes zahlenmäßig überlegene amerikanische Armee wurde letzlich besiegt und vom Feld getrieben, doch erlitt das kleine britische Heer von General Cornwallis dabei so schwere Verluste, daß es die Amerikaner nicht verfolgen und vernichten konnte.

K 21st Foot im Lager, Roermond, Holland, 1748. Als der österreichische Erbfolgekrieg im Frühjahr 1748 seinem erschöpften Ende zuging, besuchte der Schweizer Künstler David Morier das britische Heer in seinem Lager in Roermond in Holland. Sinn und Zweck seiner Reise war es, den ihm vom Herzog von Cumberland erteilten Auftrag, nämlich einen Kavalleriesoldaten und einen Grenadier aus jedem Regiment des Heers zu malen, zu erfüllen.

L Gefreiter, 1/Royals, 1789. 1 Obgleich ein Grenadier, wie an seinen Schulterklappen mit Litze erkennbar ist, trägt er einen gewöhnlichen Dreispitz anstatt der unbeliebten Bärenfellmütze, die 1768 verordnet worden war. Er ist mit einer Muskete des kurzen Landmodells und einem Bajonett bewaffnet. 2 Brustplatten des Regiments: (a) Offizier der 1/Royals; (b) Gefreiter der 1/Royals und Knopfschlaufe aus Regimentslitze. Auf dem Knopf selbst befand sich die Aufschrift FO1OT. 3 Breeches: Normalerweise waren sie aus weißer Wolle, konnten bei wärmerem Wetter jedoch durch leichtere Kleidung aus Segeltuch oder Leinen ersetzt werden. Man beachte den verdeckten Schlitz, der im Rahmen der Vorschriften von 1768 an die Stelle des Hosenschlitzes trat. 4 Hemd mit typischen Manschettenknöpfen, die aus zwei Knöpfen bestehen. 5 Halbgamaschen, wie die leichte Infanterie trug sowie andere Soldaten bei warmem Wetter oder langen Märschen. 6 Schnallenschuhe. 7 Bajonettscheide und Gürtel.

D1362958

Planetary/Authority: Ruling the World
Writer – Warren Ellis
Penciler – Phil Jimenez
Inker – Andy Lanning
(with thanks to Phil Jimenez)
Colorist – Laura DePuy Martin
Letters – Ryan Cline

Planetary/JLA: Terra Occulta
Writer – Warren Ellis
Artist – Jerry Ordway
Colorist – David Baron
Letters – Mike Heisler

Planetary/Batman: Night on Earth
Writer – Warren Ellis
Artist – John Cassaday
Colorist – David Baron
Letters – Comicraft's Wes Abbott

Cover Art - Cassaday/Martin
Collected Edition Design – Ed Roeder

Planetary created by
Warren Ellis and John Cassaday
Batman created by Bob Kane

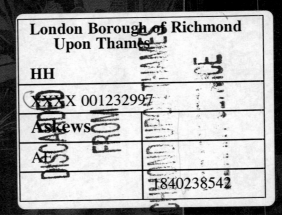

Jim Lee ▸ Editorial Director

John Nee ▸ VP & General Manager

Scott Dunbier ▸ Executive Editor

John Layman and Scott Dunbier ▸ Editors—Original Series

Kristy Quinn ▸ Assistant Editor

Robbin Brosterman ▸ Senior Art Director

Ed Roeder ▸ Art Director

Paul Levitz ▸ President & Publisher

Georg Brewer ▸ VP—Design & Retail Product Development

Richard Bruning ▸ Senior VP—Creative Director

Patrick Caldon ▸ Senior VP—Finance & Operations

Chris Caramalis ▸ VP—Finance

Terri Cunningham ▸ VP—Managing Editor

Dan DiDio ▸ VP—Editorial

Alison Gill ▸ VP—Manufacturing

Lillian Laserson ▸ Senior VP & General Counsel

David McKillips ▸ VP—Advertising & Custom Publishing

Gregory Noveck ▸ Senior VP—Creative Affairs

Cheryl Rubin ▸ VP—Brand Management

Bob Wayne ▸ VP—Sales & Marketing

CHAPTER 1

RULING THE WORLD

AND WHEN THIS APPALLING VISION PASSED, I FOUND... WELL...

MR. SNOW, I BELIEVE THESE TO BE NEGRO EGGS.

WISH I COULD SEE YOUR CONTAINMENT FIELD. DON'T TRUST IT IF I CAN'T SEE IT. IS IT GOOD?

OF COURSE IT IS. IT'S A STORM WALL. AND WHAT'S COMING IS ONLY RAIN.

IT'S A RED STICKY HAIL OF SMASHED ALIEN OCTOPUS, DOCTOR...

SHUT UP. SHAMANIC MOMENTS ARE POETIC. IF I SAY IT'S RAIN, IT'S RAIN.

WHAT HAPPENS IF YOU DON'T SAY IT'S RAIN?

THEN THE CONTAINMENT FIELD COLLAPSES AND WE DIE UNDER A MASSIVE HAIL OF BURST EVIL OCTO-MAMA.

LIGHT SUMMER RAIN.

RIGHT.

# THE CARRIER:

SAILING THE SHORE OF THE BLEED, WHERE BABY UNIVERSES ARE SPAWNED...

I KNOW THE BASTARD'S FACE FROM SOMEWHERE.

CARRIER; SHOW ME MY FAVORITE SPOT IN THE ADIRONDACKS.

NOTHING THERE. JUST CHOPPERS.

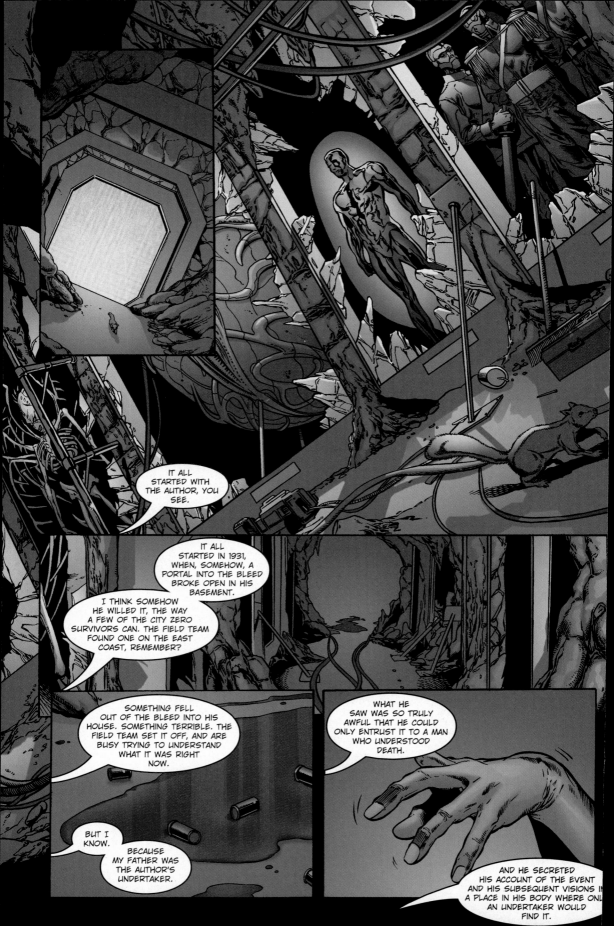

THIS THING'S FIFTY MILES WIDE AND THIRTY-FIVE MILES DEEP.

AND WE'RE AT THE BACK AND THEY'RE AT THE FRONT.

MAD.

OH, SHUSH, ELIJAH.

THEY WON'T HEAR US AND WON'T SEE US. WE JUST NEED TO TAP THEIR COMPUTER NETWORK AND GET OUT.

WHICH IS WHY I BROUGHT COMPUTER MONKEY HERE.

COMPUTER MONKEY DOESN'T DO FIELD TRIPS.

DOES COMPUTER MONKEY WANT HIS LUNGS KICKED OUT?

IF IT MEANS COMPUTER MONKEY DOESN'T HAVE TO STAY IN INCREDIBLY DANGEROUS LOCATION -- SURE, KICK 'EM OUT.

LOOK. THERE ARE PLACES WE'D ALL RATHER BE. BUT AS FAR AS I'M CONCERNED, SUCKING THEIR DATA BANKS DRY IS AN ETHICAL ACT.

THESE PEOPLE FOUGHT OFF AN INVASION FROM A PARALLEL EARTH, RE-INVADED THAT WORLD AND DESTROYED THEIR RULING POWER IN LESS THAN TWENTY-FOUR HOURS.

THE AUTHORITY MAY AS WELL BE OUR RULING POWER. AND I THINK WE NEED TO KNOW ALL ABOUT THEM IF THAT'S THE CASE.

HOLD IT. GOT A NETWORK SPUR HERE.

THAT'S ALL I NEED TO GET INTO THEIR MAINFRAME. HOPEFULLY WITHOUT LETTING THEM KNOW I'M HERE.

SHUT DOWN THE COMPUTER, DRUMS.

I SWEAR. DOC BRASS LAID IN HERE FOR FIFTY FOUR YEARS, IN CASE SOMETHING ELSE CAME OUT OF THE SNOWFLAKE.

IT'S SWITCHED ON ONCE SINCE THEN, AND LOOK...

YEAH. LOOK.

SOUNDS LIKE THE AUTHORITY'S ARRIVED.

SOMETHING ELSE, TOO. THERE'S INFORMATION LOOSE OUT THERE. LOTS OF IT. LIKE SOMETHING SCREAMING.

SOMETHING UNDERLYING IT, TOO... SOMETHING I MIGHT BE ABLE TO HOOK INTO.

STOP YAMMERING, BOY. I'M TRYING TO THINK.

THERE IT IS. RADIOTELEPATHY.

I'M HOOKED INTO THE AUTHORITY'S PRIVATE COMMUNICATIONS CHANNEL.

JENNY, I'VE GOT ONE OF THE THINGS --

-- AND THE SHORT VERSION IS, IT'S A SELF-REPLICATING WAR ROBOT DESIGNED TO ANNEX WORLDS.

AND I COUNT ABOUT A THOUSAND OF THEM.

WHICH, ACCORDING TO THE MATH IN THIS THING'S BRAIN, MEANS THERE'LL BE TEN THOUSAND OF THEM IN ABOUT FIFTEEN MINUTES.

IT'S CALLED A **WORLDRULER**. THEY JUST DROPPED MILLIONS OF THEM INTO THE BLEED, TOLD THEM TO LOOK FOR WAYS INTO PARALLEL UNIVERSES--

--AND INVADE THOSE EARTHS AND KILL EVERY-THING FOR THEM.

IT JUST GIVES BIRTH TO DEATH-DEVICES UNTIL EVERYTHING'S DEAD. JUST STOPPING THESE ROBOTS IS ONLY HALF THE JOB--

OH, LOOK.

IT'S A JAKITA WAGNER. I *LOVE* KILLING THOSE.

THE ROBOTS ARE STARTING TO REPRODUCE!

NOW OR NEVER-- WE GET A PLAN OR THESE THINGS KILL EVERYTHING!

**END.**

CHAPTER 2

TERRA OCCULTA

But I can't, of course. You know that as well as I do. Better than I do.

I am trapped here in Man's World, a civilization I learned of through viewscreens. Nothing prepared me for the way this place feels.

The VOICES. This is a city of voices, of constant chatter. There is no song here, Mother. Only the tinny riot of untrained voices from their radios, and the clatter of their talk.

I find myself longing for the days when their cars made noise.

GRAND CENTRAL STATION, PLEASE.

CUEROZO

LIVERY

AIR GLIDE
$8.50 INITIAL CHARGE
$2.00 PER KILO
$2.00 PER MIN.
$1.00 FOR (??)

NO NO NO. YOU SEE, THE ORIGINAL TIMETRACK THEORY HAD IT THAT THE LOOP BEGINS AT THE POINT OF ACTIVATION AND PROCEEDS INTO THE FUTURE.

HOWEVER, I AM CONVINCED THAT THERE MUST BE A GHOST LOOP BACKTRACKING FROM THE ACTIVATION POINT, AND--

--AND BRUCE WAYNE PAYS FOR THIS? GOD, HE'S MORE STUPID THAN I THOUGHT.

I DON'T FEEL COMFORTABLE WITH "INVENTOR." I PREFER "TECHNOLOGIST." IT FITS BETTER WITH WONDERDOME FUTURES' BACKGROUND AND GOALS.

NO, COLLIMATING STRUCTURE AND TESSERACT TECHNOLOGY ARE THINGS MY FAMILY HAD BEEN WORKING ON IN THEORY SINCE THE 1950'S. THANKFULLY, MR. WAYNE'S MONEY--

--IS NEVER BETTER SPENT THAN ON DIANA PRINCE, AND HER WONDERS TO PERFORM.

HELLO, BRUCE

MR. WAYNE!

HERE COMES BRUCE TO SINK HIS CLAWS IN

DRUNK TOO

MR. WAYNE? YOU LOOK LIKE YOU'RE WONDERING ABOUT SOMETHING.

MM.

I WAS WONDERING WHAT IT'D BE LIKE TO...

NO, LET ME PUT IT THIS WAY.

I WAS WONDERING IF I COULD TAKE YOU HOME.

I'VE ALWAYS WANTED TO SEE STATELY WAYNE MANOR.

AFTER YOU, MS. PRINCE, PLEASE.

CHIVALRY IS NOT DEAD.

NO, JUST LAYING DOWN FOR A WHILE. WHICH, YOU MUST ADMIT, IS AN EXCELLENT IDEA.

ALFRED. STATUS?

ALL SECURITY SYSTEMS ON; NOTHING INSIDE THE GROUNDS CAN BE SEEN OR HEARD FROM ABOVE, SIR.

GOOD. HOW DID YOU GET HERE, DIANA?

I TOOK A DOOR FROM NEW YORK.

DIANA, YOU SHOULDN'T USE THE DOORS, THEY MONITOR THEM. IF THEY'D CAUGHT YOU USING THEM, THEY COULD'VE TELEPORTED YOU FIVE MILES DOWN.

BRUCE, WE'RE ALL WELL AWARE BY NOW THAT THEY KEEP ME ALIVE BECAUSE IT AMUSES THEM TO DO SO.

STILL, YOU SHOULD TAKE MORE CARE. IF I COULD FIND YOU, THEY COULD FIND YOU.

WHAT ABOUT CLARK?

THEIR SURVEILLANCE SATELLITES WILL BE IN THE PREDICTED CONJUNCTION IN ABOUT THREE MINUTES, MASTER BRUCE.

CONJUNCTION?

I PLANNED THE PARTY TO TAKE ADVANTAGE OF IT. EVERY FEW DAYS, THE SATELLITES' ORBITS ACCIDENTALLY CREATE A CORRIDOR OF UNMONITORED AIRSPACE BETWEEN HERE AND METROPOLIS.

IT LASTS ABOUT SIX MINUTES. I THINK THAT'LL MAKE AN INTERESTING POWERS TEST FOR MR. KENT.

COFFEE?

THE CORRIDOR OPENED UP A LITTLE OVER THREE MINUTES AGO.

LET'S SEE.

AHA.

EXCELLENT. NEARLY THERE, MR. KENT, NEARLY THERE...

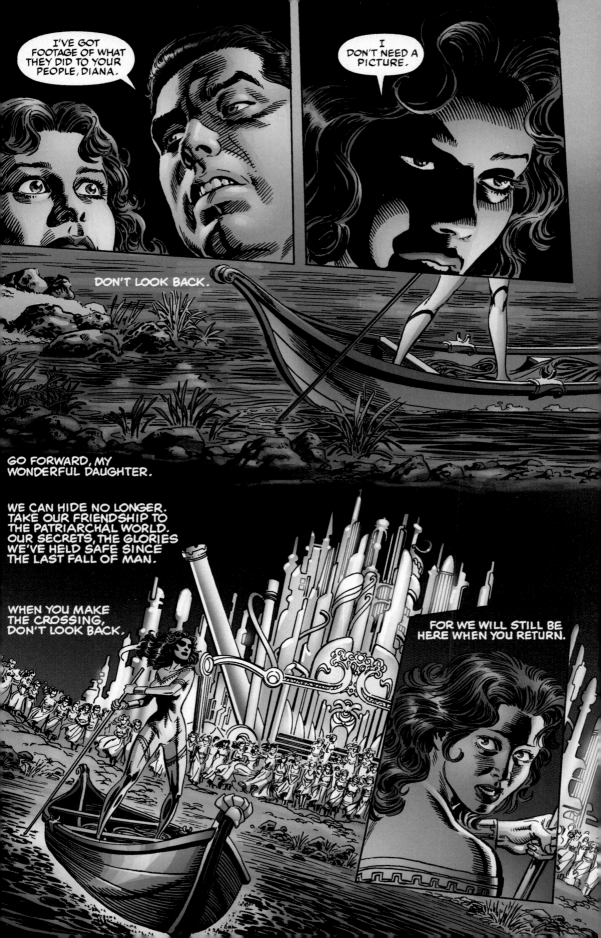

...BUT I PLAN AHEAD WHEREVER POSSIBLE. I HAVE BODY ARMOR IN THE BACK FOR YOU BOTH, IF YOU'RE SURE YOU'RE...

I DON'T NEED IT.

AND I HAVE EVERYTHING I NEED RIGHT HERE.

SO WHAT'S THIS ERDEL DOING?

TIME PHYSICS.

AMBROSE CHASE.

YES, WHAT MAKES MR. CHASE SO FORMIDABLE IS HIS LOCALIZED PHYSICS-DISTORTION FIELD.

IN FACT, I SUSPECT CHASE'S VERY PUBLIC "POLICE ACTION" AGAINST GABRIEL WALKER IN 1995 GAVE ERDEL THE INSPIRATION.

WALKER'S "TIME GAUNTLETS" ARE, OF COURSE, NOW IN THE PLANETARY WATCHTOWER ON THE MOON.

I DID SOME DIGGING ON WALKER. HE WAS NO TERRORIST. THE BOMB IN SAN FRANCISCO THAT HE SUPPOSEDLY PLANTED WASN'T HIS.

NO, HE WAS, IN FACT, ATTEMPTING TO USE HIS TIME-TRAVEL DEVICE TO PUMP THE BOMB INTO THE PAST, SO THAT IT WOULD HAVE EXPLODED IN SPACE, BEHIND THE EARTH.

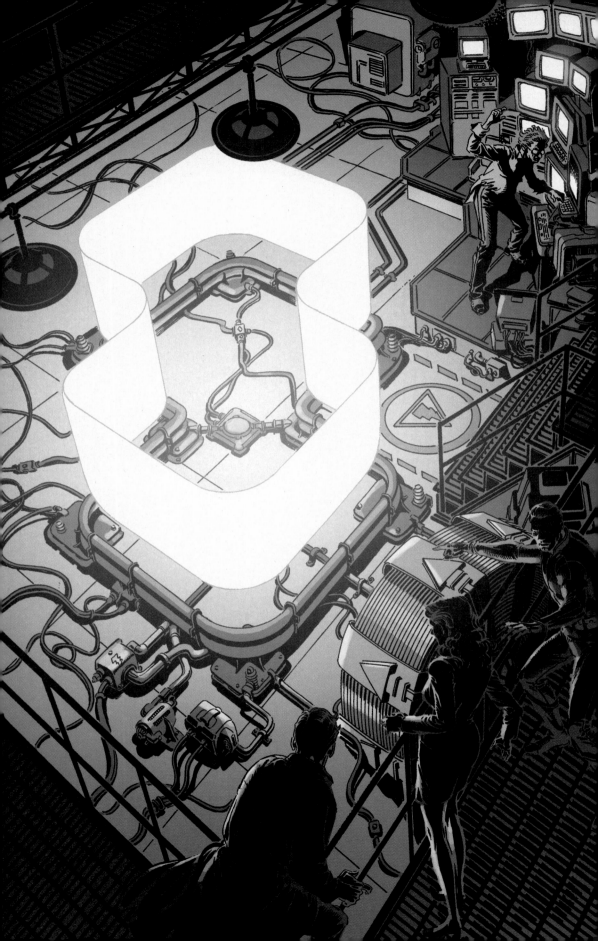

WHAT IS THAT?

IT'S A TIME LOOP.

PHYSICS IS BENT DOUBLE INSIDE THE LOOP.

THE LIGHT CUTS A CHANNEL INTO THE FUTURE AND THEN COMES SCREAMING BACK.

STAND AT THE START POINT OF THE LOOP AND TAKE THREE STEPS FORWARD.

STEP OUT OF THE LOOP AND YOU'RE A YEAR IN THE FUTURE.

STEP BACK IN AND WALK BACK TO THE PRESENT.

I DON'T LIKE THE LOOK OF THE LIGHT.

HOW SO?

TOO BRIGHT, TOO MUCH POWER.

HOLD IT, THE AMBIENT NOISE FROM OUTSIDE JUST STOPPED. I CAN STILL HEAR THE CARS, BUT...

STAND BACK, I CAN SEE THROUGH WALLS, BUT THERE'S A SMALL ATTENDANT X-RAY OVERSPLASH.

THE LIGHTS JUST WENT OUT OVER HALF OF GOTHAM.

HE'S ATTACHED THE CITY GRID TO POWER HIS MACHINE.

PERHAPS IT'LL KILL AMBROSE CHASE, TOO.

IT CERTAINLY GOT DR. ERDEL.

ANOTHER WONDER LOST.

AND ONE GAINED. A PLANETARY MOBILE PORTAL GENERATOR.

WE DON'T HAVE MUCH TIME. AS SOON AS CHASE IS MISSED, THEY'LL DEACTIVATE THE DEVICE REMOTELY.

WE HAVE TO USE THIS NOW OR NOT AT ALL.

DIRECTLY INTO THE PLANETARY WATCHTOWER?

DIRECTLY. DIRECTLY TO THE MOON.

AND NO WAY BACK.

ONLY IF WE LOSE.

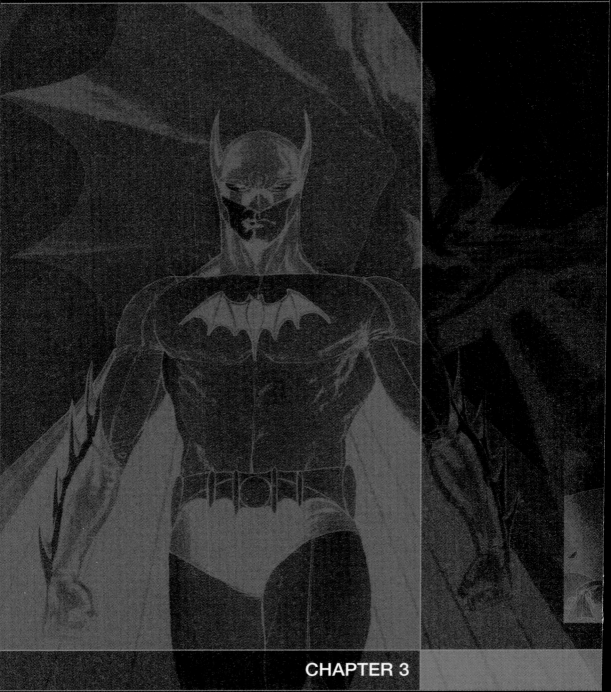

CHAPTER 3

NIGHT ON EARTH

WHAT ARE THESE COMING TOWARDS US?

LOCAL PLANETARY OFFICE STAFF. THEY'RE A BIT ENTHUSIASTIC. TRY NOT TO BITE THEIR HEADS OFF.

ELIJAH SNOW, THIS IS DICK GRAYSON, HEAD OF THE LOCAL OFFICE--

--AND THIS IS JASPER, HIS ASSISTANT.

I, AH, HI, YES, ME, OFFICE, HI. *HI.*

COOL. *HA HA.* VERY COOL. *HA.* COOL.

AND, AH, I JUST WANTED TO, YOU KNOW, *SAY,* MISS WAGNER, *JAKITA,* YOU'RE LOOKING BEAUTIFUL, AND SEXY, AND EXCELLENT AND GORGEOUS AS, YOU KNOW, *EVER...*

HA.

DON'T BITE THEIR HEADS OFF.

JUST BE, YOU KNOW, COOL. VERY COOL. AND BEAUTIFUL AND SEXY AND EXCELLENT AND GORGEOUS.

LET'S GO.

DICK.

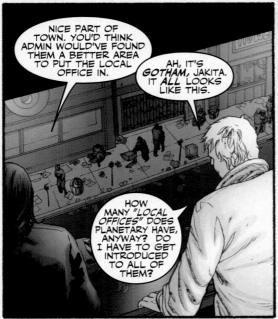

NICE PART OF TOWN. YOU'D THINK ADMIN WOULD'VE FOUND THEM A BETTER AREA TO PUT THE LOCAL OFFICE IN.

AH, IT'S *GOTHAM*, JAKITA. IT *ALL* LOOKS LIKE THIS.

HOW MANY *"LOCAL OFFICES"* DOES PLANETARY HAVE, ANYWAY? DO I HAVE TO GET INTRODUCED TO ALL OF THEM?

WELL, IT'S NOT CALLED PLANETARY BECAUSE WE ONLY HAVE OFFICES IN TWOBLONDES, ARIZONA.

IT'S A BIG JOB WE SET OURSELVES: UNCOVERING THE SECRET HISTORY OF THE WORLD.

SO WE'RE ALL OVER THE PLANET: DIGGING EVERYWHERE AT ONCE.

AH, MISS WAGNER...THE DRUMMER'S DOING SOMETHING TO MY TELEVISION SET AGAIN...

ZIP IT UP, DRUMS.

AND I'VE TOLD YOU BEFORE ABOUT MAKING INNOCENT PEOPLE'S TV SETS PICK UP SHOWS FROM OTHER PLANETS.

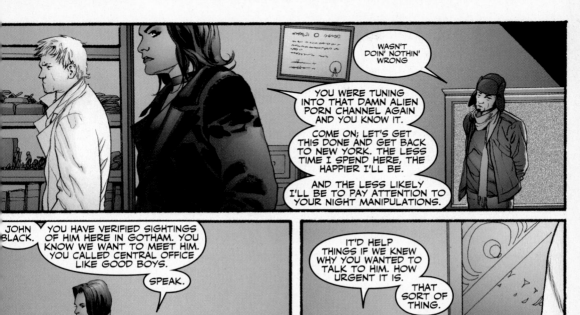

WASN'T DOIN' NOTHIN' WRONG

YOU WERE TUNING INTO THAT DAMN ALIEN PORN CHANNEL AGAIN AND YOU KNOW IT.

COME ON; LET'S GET THIS DONE AND GET BACK TO NEW YORK. THE LESS TIME I SPEND HERE, THE HAPPIER I'LL BE.

AND THE LESS LIKELY I'LL BE TO PAY ATTENTION TO YOUR NIGHT MANIPULATIONS.

JOHN BLACK. YOU HAVE VERIFIED SIGHTINGS OF HIM HERE IN GOTHAM. YOU KNOW WE WANT TO MEET HIM. YOU CALLED CENTRAL OFFICE LIKE GOOD BOYS.

SPEAK.

IT'D HELP THINGS IF WE KNEW WHY YOU WANTED TO TALK TO HIM. HOW URGENT IT IS.

THAT SORT OF THING.

WE'VE ASCERTAINED THAT HIS FATHER WAS ONE OF A HANDFUL OF SURVIVORS OF THE AMERICAN SECRET EXPERIMENTATION CAMP SCIENCE CITY ZERO.

WE'VE REASON TO BELIEVE THAT HIS FATHER'S ENHANCED GENETIC STRUCTURE WILL HAVE GIVEN JOHN SOME KIND OF SUPERHUMAN CAPABILITY.

WE WANT TO KNOW WHAT JOHN'S FATHER TOLD HIM ABOUT CITY ZERO, AND WE'D LIKE TO KNOW WHAT HE CAN DO.

KILL PEOPLE.

HE CAN KILL PEOPLE.

REPORTS OF HIM BEHAVING STRANGELY IN PUBLIC...PICKED UP ON SUSPECTED DRUG USE BY THE COPS, BOUNCED WHEN HE TESTED NEGATIVE...

...FIRST BODY WITH HIS PRINTS ON FOUND 'ROUND THE BACK OF A SOUP KITCHEN, A BLOCK FROM CRIME ALLEY.

"CRIME ALLEY." TOLD YOU. HEADS FULL OF ABSINTHE.

SHUT UP, YOU HORRIBLE OLD MAN.

SECOND KILL IS WHAT SET OUR ALARMS OFF.

IT'S EASIER IF YOU JUST LOOK AT THIS PHOTO, LET ME PIN IT ON THE RIGHT LOCATION HERE...

DAMMIT. I'VE SEEN THAT BEFORE.

1986.

WHAT HAPPENED IN 1986?

PARTIAL MULTIVERSAL COLLAPSE.

SEVERAL UNIVERSES GOT FOLDED INTO ONE-- MULTIPLE EARTHS OCCUPYING THE SAME SPACE.

THIS IS WHAT HAPPENED TO ABOUT A THIRD OF THE COMBINED POPULATION.

WHERE THE HELL WERE YOU IN 1986?

SOMEWHERE I WASN'T SUPPOSED TO BE.

OKAY. REMEMBER WHEN I SAID THAT I REALLY DON'T WANT TO GO ON ANY MORE FIELD MISSIONS?

WELL, I MEANT IT. SERIOUSLY.

STAYING HERE. REALLY STAYING HERE.

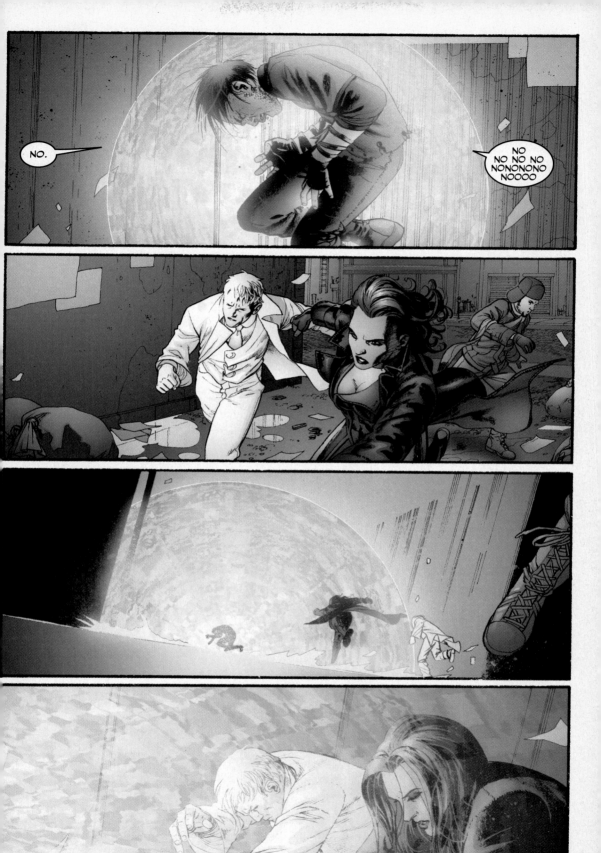

THESE AREN'T THE SAME BUILDINGS WE STOOD UNDER A MOMENT AGO.

THE IMMEDIATE SKYLINE'S DIFFERENT. THAT GRATING WASN'T THERE A SECOND AGO.

DRUMS? YOU OKAY?

ALL THE INFORMATION PATTERNS JUST...*CHANGED*, JAKITA.

ALL THE CELLPHONE FREQUENCIES, ALL THE TV SIGNALS... IT WAS LIKE HAVING SOMEONE RIP OUT YOUR EYES AND SHOVE NEW ONES IN.

THIS IS REALLY, REALLY SCREWED UP.

OH MY GOD.

NOT AS SORRY AS YOU'RE GOING TO BE.

SNOW! INCOMING!

THERE'S SOME KIND OF TRANSVESTITE HOOKER RUNNING DOWN THE ALLEYWAY AT US.

IT'S THE CAPE GUY, ISN'T IT?

BLACK'S CHANGE-FIELD SURGED AND WE SHIFTED PLACES AGAIN. THAT'S ANOTHER ITERATION OF CAPE GUY.

TRY AND GET BLACK UP ON HIS FEET.

I'VE GOT CAPE GUY.

EEEAAAAAA

OH, GOD...

OKAY, GIVE ME A SECOND, LET ME JUST--

HE'S A KILLER.

HE'S SICK. HE'S BARELY IN HIS OWN HEAD.

THEREFORE HE'S NOT GETTING TURNED OVER TO GOTHAM COPS, AND WE'RE NOT HANDING HIM TO A GUY DRESSED AS A BAT.

IN MY CITY-- IN THIS PLACE-- I AM NOT LETTING A MURDERER GO FREE.

AND HE'S NOT GOING TO GO FREE. BUT THERE IS MORE THAN YOUR MORAL WHATEVERITIS AT STAKE HERE.

NO, THERE ISN'T.

LOOK BOTH WAYS BEFORE CROSSING THE STREET.

IF YOU'RE SICK, IT'S ARKHAM ASYLUM FOR YOU.

BUT YOU'RE GOING TO MEET COMMISSIONER GORDON'S BOYS FIRST, REGARDLESS.

SORRY.

HURTS.

OF COURSE IT HURTS. YOU'VE BEEN RUN OVER.

NO.

WHAT I DID. NOT ME.

DIDN'T MEAN TO.

I DON'T BELIEVE IT.

THE DRUMMER FINALLY GETS PUNCHED INTO UNCONSCIOUSNESS AND I DIDN'T GET TO DO IT.

TOO MANY PIECES OF MY BRAIN WORKING AT ONCE.

BAD STUFF COMES OUT.

NOT ME. DIDN'T MEAN TO.

DO YOU UNDERSTAND EVEN A LITTLE OF WHAT HE'S TELLING YOU?

THEY HAVE GOOD PEOPLE AT ARKHAM. THEY'LL WORK IT OUT.

I DON'T THINK SO.

WHAT WE CALL "REALITY" IS AN ARRAY OF 196,833 PARALLEL UNIVERSES ARRANGED IN A SNOWFLAKE PATTERN.

THAT MAN, AND HIS PARENTS, WERE MUTILATED IN AN EXPERIMENTAL CONCENTRATION CAMP.

THE RESULT OF HIS TORTURE IS A BRAIN LOCKED INTO THE MOTION OF THE MULTIVERSE.

HE CAN'T COPE WITH IT.

IT'S DRIVEN HIM INSANE.

THEY WERE KILLED.

...DOESN'T MATTER.

HE HAS TO BE BROUGHT TO JUSTICE.

YES. BUT BY US.

AAAAAAAAAAAAAAAAAAAA

OH, GOD.

YOU'RE NOT A COP, ARE YOU?

I DON'T THINK VIGILANTE IS THE RIGHT WORD, EITHER.

WHAT'S YOUR NAME?

JOHN BLACK.

HOW DID YOUR PARENTS DIE?

THEY WERE SHOT.

WHAT ARE YOUR INTENTIONS?

THE PEOPLE WHO KILLED HIS PARENTS KILLED MANY OTHER PEOPLE. AND LEFT DAMAGED GOODS LIKE HIM BEHIND.

HIS MEMORIES WILL GIVE US VITAL CLUES TO TRACKING THOSE PEOPLE DOWN.

AND BRINGING *THEM* TO JUSTICE.

THEY'RE THE CRIMINALS HERE.

IT'S YOUR PANIC THAT'S DOING THIS?

YOU'VE LOST CONTROL, AND IT'S CAUSING THIS ROTATION EFFECT THEY'RE TALKING ABOUT.

THAT WAS YOU, WASN'T IT? THE LITTLE BOY?

HOW DO YOU DO IT?

HOW DO YOU COPE?

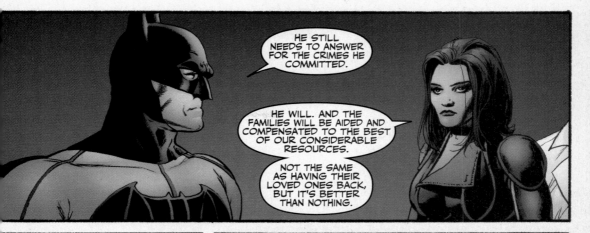

HE STILL NEEDS TO ANSWER FOR THE CRIMES HE COMMITTED.

HE WILL. AND THE FAMILIES WILL BE AIDED AND COMPENSATED TO THE BEST OF OUR CONSIDERABLE RESOURCES.

NOT THE SAME AS HAVING THEIR LOVED ONES BACK, BUT IT'S BETTER THAN NOTHING.

WE'RE ROTATING BACK.. HE'S RELAXED.

I'M TRUSTING YOU TO DO THE RIGHT THING.

I DON'T CARE IF YOU'RE FROM MY "REALITY" OR NOT--THIS IS STILL MY CITY.

AND I'LL FIND YOU IF I HAVE TO.

I TOTALLY BEAT YOU UP, YOU KNOW.

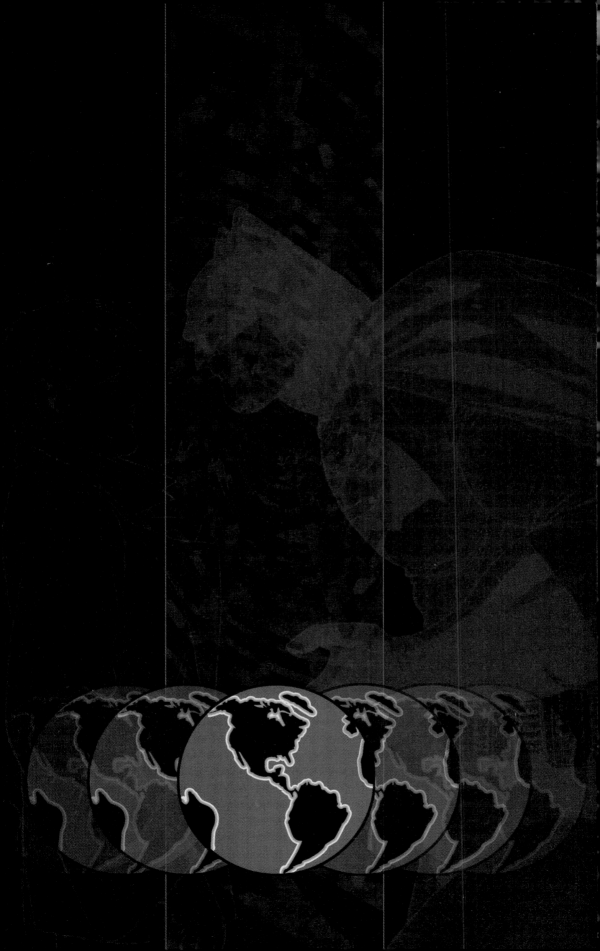

**ORIGINAL COVER CONCEPTS FOR TERRA OCCULTA**

JLA/PLANETARY SKETCH #3

#4 JLA REFLECTED IN PUDDLE

#5

#6

SPOOKY WAYNE MANOR

BY JERRY ORDWAY

**PLANETARY:
VOLUMES 1 & 2**

ELLIS/CASSADAY

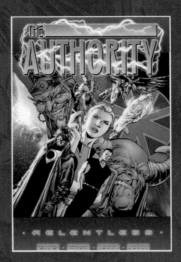

**THE AUTHORITY:
RELENTLESS**

ELLIS/HITCH/NEARY

**STORMWATCH:
CHANGE OR DIE**

ELLIS/RANEY/JIMENEZ

**DV8:
NEIGHBORHOOD THREAT**

ELLIS/RAMOS/REGLA

**GLOBAL FREQUENCY:
PLANET ABLAZE**

ELLIS/VARIOUS

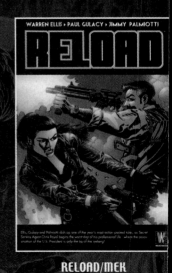

**RELOAD/MEK**

ELLIS/GULACY & ELLIS/ROLSTON

# Other books of interest by Warren Ellis

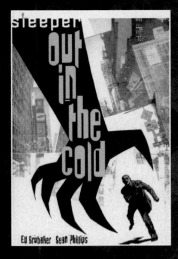

**BATMAN/DEATHBLOW:
AFTER THE FIRE**

AZZARELLO/BERMEJO

**THE MONARCHY:
BULLETS OVER BABYLON**

YOUNG/McCREA/LEACH/PLEECE

**SLEEPER:
OUT IN THE COLD**

BRUBAKER/PHILLIPS

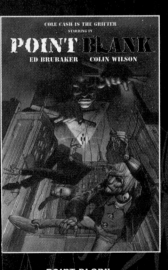

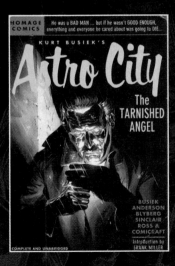

**POINT BLANK**

BRUBAKER/WILSON

**TOP10:
BOOKS 1 & 2**

MOORE/HA/CANNON

**THE ASTRO CITY LIBRARY**

BUSIEK/ANDERSON/BLYBERG

# Other books of interest by WildStorm/ABC

To find more collected editions and monthly comic books from WildStorm and DC Comics, call
**1-888-comic book for the nearest comics shop**
or go to your local book store.